The Famous New Englanders Cookbook

The Famous New Englanders Cookbook

YANKEE® BOOKS

A division of Yankee Publishing Incorporated
Dublin, New Hampshire

Edited by Sandra J. Taylor
Designed by Jill Shaffer
Illustrated by Bruce Hammond

Yankee Publishing Incorporated
Dublin, New Hampshire
First Edition
Copyright 1984 by
Yankee Publishing Incorporated

Library of Congress Catalogue Card Number 84-50426
ISBN 0-89909-037-0 (hardcover)
ISBN 0-89909-039-7 (softcover)

Table of Contents

Foreword

*I*f you're not in the mood for surprises, then close this book forthwith and search your library for something safe. Something bland like cream of wheat with milk and sugar. Something that will protect you from the ecstatic heights of emotional peaks and the depths of emotional valleys. Because when a book devotes itself to food and eating, that, in itself, is toying dangerously with those mysterious feelings called "hungers" emanating daily from our individual psyches. But when there's the additional ingredient, as there is in this book, of asking certain individuals to confess to their *favorite* method of temporarily satiating *their* own particular brand of secret hunger, well, readers had best brace themselves.

The afternoon that editor Sandy Taylor handed me a copy of *The Famous New Englanders Cookbook,* then in rough manuscript form, I flipped open directly to Margaret Manning's "Stuffed Roast Leg of Lamb." I don't believe I would have confessed to that one, Margaret. It sounds far too sinfully, luxuriously delicious! I mean, that one cup of brown stock alone contains beef shanks, veal shanks, sliced onions, carrots, salt, parsley, and thyme and that is added to wine, sliced onion, rosemary, salt, pepper, "and whatever" before we even begin to address the butterflied lamb. Surely the addition of "whatever" represents a few mysteries that Margaret has probably never confessed even to herself.

Oh, my, I thought, this is a book of dreams. Would I ever meet Margaret Manning and would she ever share with me exactly what she's described, including all her "whatevers"? If so, could I survive and go on living a normal life after experiencing Margaret's recipe for "Stuffed Roast Leg of Lamb"? Probably not. Yes, I decided, this is surely a book of dreams.

Robert Brustein shook me awake. I mean anybody — even I! — can make scrambled eggs like *that,* Robert. His favorite recipe is dropping a few eggs in a bowl, adding salt, pepper, and dill, stirring with a fork, and then putting 'em in a butter-greased frying pan until they're ready to eat. That's no dream. That's *life!* Ah, but I noticed Robert had another favorite that he calls his "Seduction Dinner." Curiously, I flipped through more pages to determine how many others possessed the raw courage to tell the general reading public that love and food often intertwined in the inner machinations of *their* particular hungers. Congratulations to Maxwell Mays. I've always known Max to be a fearless fellow.

Interesting to compare their two roads to seduction, though. Max obviously feels it should be fairly short — no soup or salad is mentioned and his entire seduction dish, "Chicken Sauté Archiduc," served with "the thinnest slices of cucumber," takes only twenty minutes but "needs constant attention." He advises against answering the telephone during this period.

Robert takes the longer road. He begins with generous helpings of very dry Stolichnaya martinis followed by vichyssoise, garlic bread, salad, and pan-fried filet mignon with artichokes. The ending (of the meal) is a piece of Sara Lee cake (a consistent craving from childhood, no doubt), coffee, and VSOP cognac.

I'm reasonably sure that the roads of both Max and Robert invariably lead to something or other rather intriguing. Why else would they list them as "favorites"? However, I'm reminded of Clifton Fadiman's observation concerning certain foods or meals as aphrodisiacs. "The only dependable aphrodisiacs . . .," he once wrote, "are not to be found in books. They are two in number, the first being the presence of a desirable woman, the second her absence." I assume the quote is equally true with the genders reversed.

To know that Tip O'Neill enjoys "Cape Cod Fish Chowder" at Jimmy's Harborside Restaurant when he's in Boston neither surprises nor intrigues me. No offense, Mr. Speaker. But the late Buckminster Fuller's favorite, "Cream of Tomato Ice Cream," is as inventive and intriguing as the geodesic dome.

Some of the surprises aren't the actual recipes as much as *whose* favorites they are. For instance, I might be tempted to predict that Margaret Chase Smith's true love is a pot of Boston baked beans but, somehow, not Father Drinan's. I can well imagine the late Scott Nearing munching oats and raisins moistened with vegetable oil. (Equally dreadful, or worse, is Dr. Benjamin Spock's contribution, which is virtually the same as Scott Nearing's but without raisins and using water instead of oil. Dr. Spock could have been the only happy inmate of a Japanese prison camp during the last world war.) However, I wonder what unknown subliminal forces are at work in the hunger mechanisms of musicians when three of them in this book, James Bolle, Leonard Bernstein, and Tammy Grimes, appear helpless to control their strong desires for lemons.

I might add that Robert J. Lurtsema's favorites are the only ones that always represent a surprise even to Robert J. Lurtsema! Cooking totally "by instinct," he uses whatever ingredients seem best to fit "the impulse of the moment," saying that, to him, "gustatory ecstasy is an ephemeral experience."

Not so for most of us. Favorite dishes are deep-seated, lifetime longings occasionally interrupted by a heavenly gorging of the physical manifestation of said culinary fantasy. Rather than, as with Robert J. Lurtsema, it always be different, it is important to many that it always be the same.

"This is good," John Cole might say as he digs into a piece of "Seven-Layer Mocha Cake," his passion since childhood days, "but it's not quite like my wife's recipe for it." John gives us another tiny, but oh-so-revealing, clue to his marvelous obsession with "Seven-Layer Mocha Cake" when he confides that "as far as health benefits, the cake hasn't one redeeming feature, which is another reason why it's my favorite." Thanks, John. Now we can all confess. There's no question in my mind that a dash of wickedness invariably enhances sensory experiences.

Am I the only one in the world, for instance, who finds himself drifting quietly, unobtrusively, from the dining room into the kitchen after a hearty meal for the sole purpose of delicately plucking from the still-warm frying pan two or three of those exquisite little burnt morsels of happiness called "dregs"? So greasy and salty and crunchy. And so wicked. I confess that a lifelong fantasy of mine is to prepare an entire meal of frying-pan dregs. I'll concede, however, the possibility that the limited number of decent dregs remaining in a frying pan could contribute to and exaggerate their intense attractiveness. In other words, an *abundance* of frying-pan dregs, i.e. all one could eat, might destroy the delicate balance of psychological elements that mix together in precisely the correct proportions to produce the delightful compulsion I, for one, presently enjoy.

Stephen King undoubtedly understands. Steve, your "favorite" — consisting of two cans of Franco American Spaghetti mixed with a pound of "cheap, greasy hamburger," preferably somewhat scorched in a frying pan and served with buttered Wonder Bread — is a lovely, if somewhat scary, revelation. I'm not certain something *that* intimate should be divulged to the entire world, though. Nonetheless, you honor us in the extreme by so doing. Here. Right in this book.

So now, if you've read this far, prepare, please, to know more about some famous New Englanders than you ever thought possible. You'll find yourself uplifted in their culinary exultations, depressed by occasional excursions into banality. Your cheeks will ache and it's remotely possible your stomach will fleetingly turn. You'll find that the secret dreams of some will coincide with your own and that the fantasies of others will simmer within you to eventually create deliciously *new* longings in your heart. Above all, remember that the following recipes are personal favorites and are not, therefore, subject to judicative decisions relative to good or bad. We're not concerned with what they are, but rather that they are.

Proceed, if you wish to be so bold . . . .

Judson D. Hale, Sr.
Editor, *Yankee* magazine and
The Old Farmer's Almanac

A-C

Clockwise from top: Mary Cunningham, Leonard Bernstein, Frank Avruch, Cleveland Amory

Thomas Boylston Adams

Author and historian

*D*irect descendant of John Adams and John Quincy Adams, Thomas Boylston Adams is, among many other things, a widely published writer and treasurer of the American Academy of Arts and Sciences. He and his wife, Ramelle, have five children and live in Lincoln, Massachusetts.

"I was born in Kansas City, Missouri — my mother in Topeka, Kansas — so I am a real American. Came to live in Lincoln, Massachusetts, at the age of three so I suppose I am an adopted New Englander — almost a Yankee. Went to Boise, Idaho, to fight the war and ended up in Salina, Kansas, at a B29 base to reaffirm my American citizenship. Returned to Lincoln in 1946 and went to work in Boston on State Street where I have been trying ever since to acquire the status and the fortune of a Brahmin."

CORN BREAD

"For some reason, quite unknown, most Adamses have been good cooks.
My father was a superb cook. He used to bring out fish very often from
Boston and if it was to be broiled like fresh mackerel, he always built a fire
in the fireplace, reduced it to red hardwood coals and then broiled the
mackerel over the coals. My father's particular and most famous receipt was
of what we called corn bread. It was a hard corn bread about a quarter of
an inch thick. It had to be begun every spring by planting hard field corn.
This corn my father personally cultivated. In October the ears were
harvested and husked, shucked is the word, then all winter long my father
would shell the corn by hand as he needed it. Then he would grind it by
hand every morning before breakfast. The receipt was simple. Take a flat
pan about 12″ x 8″, melt some butter in the bottom, let the butter harden in
the ice chest, then spread a batter over it made of cornmeal, a little salt and
sufficient water to form a thick paste. Put the pan with the batter in it in the
oven at somewhere between 350 and 400 degrees and cook for about 15
minutes. The result is real corn bread, very much like the corn bread the
Pilgrims used to eat when they sat around Plymouth Rock. They used the
simple Indian receipt. Heat a big rock, the flattest rock available, by
building a fire around and over it. When the rock is good and hot, scrape
away the fire, mix cornmeal and water in a bucket. Then take it by the
handful, slap it on the rock. In ten minutes you have plenty of delicious
corn bread. This is how real corn bread, New England style, is made. If you
live on it as I have for more than 70 years, your teeth are as good today as
when your second crop came in. 'The sound of the grinders is not low. The
grinders do not cease because they are few.' [See Ecclesiastes 12:1-4] I am all
for remembering your creator in the days of your youth but your youth will
last longer if you bake and eat real corn bread. The great modern difficulty
is that it is almost impossible to get good cornmeal. You can get a fair
substitute for the old-time stuff at some of the nature food stores."

Cleveland Amory

Writer, lecturer, and social historian

 leveland Amory was born in the Boston resort of Nahant ("a place which, if you were not born there, you are mispronouncing"), and is of a long line of Boston merchants and Harvard graduates. After attending Milton Academy, he too went to Harvard, where he was president of the *Crimson,* a job he described as "meaning so much that, while life afterward does go on, it's never quite the same thing." From there he went to work for the *Saturday Evening Post,* as associate editor.

Mr. Amory has been free-lancing since 1947, during which time he has written a number of books (including *The Proper Bostonians*) and contributed regularly to a variety of magazines, *Saturday Review, TV Guide, Cosmopolitan,* and *Town and Country,* among others. In 1967 he founded The Fund for Animals, a society that works for the protection of all animals. The recipes Mr. Amory contributed are for vegetarian dishes which he feels are not only delicious but can be enjoyed without wondering what, if anything, was ill-treated in the production.

ACORN SQUASH CASSEROLE

4 medium acorn squash	½ cup chopped parsley
2 ounces soybean margarine	2 cups mushrooms
4 sweet potatoes	1 teaspoon paprika
½ cup chopped onions	Salt to taste
½ cup vegetable oil	

Cut each acorn squash in half — cleaning out seeds. Spread each half with soybean margarine. Wrap halves individually in foil and bake until soft, about 30 minutes. Bake sweet potatoes about 30 minutes or till done. Sauté onions in vegetable oil. Add ¼ cup parsley. Add mushrooms, paprika, and dash of salt. Scoop out squash and arrange in large oiled baking dish. Layer with sweet potatoes and mushrooms. Garnish with remaining parsley, paprika, and soybean margarine — to melt. Salt to taste. Bake in well-heated oven for 12 minutes.

Serves 4.

Vegetarian Chili

⅓ cup olive oil
2 cups chopped onion
2 green peppers, chopped
5 cloves garlic, minced
½ cup sliced celery
2 cans (26 ounces each) tomatoes (about 3 pounds, preferably San Marzano variety tomato)
8 to 10 ounces (to taste) canned green chillis, drained and minced
3 cups chopped carrots
2 small zucchini
1 to 2 teaspoons crushed dried pepper
1 to 2 teaspoons oregano
Salt to taste
2 pounds canned red kidney beans, drained
1 pound canned pinto beans, drained
Chopped cashews (optional)

In large pot heat oil over medium heat. Add onion and green peppers. Cook until tender, stirring occasionally. Add garlic. Stir in remaining ingredients, except beans. Stir occasionally, breaking up tomatoes. Cook over medium heat for about 30 minutes. Add beans. Cook 30 minutes. Serve over hot brown rice. Garnish with chopped unsalted cashews, if desired.

Serves 10.

Stuffed Mushrooms

20 medium mushrooms
½ cup chopped onions
2 tablespoons olive oil
3 garlic cloves, minced
¼ cup chopped parsley
½ cup bread crumbs
1 pound of fresh spinach, finely chopped and steamed
Nutmeg

Remove stems from mushrooms and chop. Sauté onions in pan with olive oil. Add garlic and parsley. Mix in rest of ingredients except nutmeg. Stuff mushroom caps. Sprinkle with nutmeg. Bake for 20 minutes in well-oiled baking dish.

Continued

Cleveland Amory *continued*

RATATOUILLE PROVENÇALE

1 medium eggplant
1 cup light olive oil
1 pound plum tomatoes
1 jar (4 ounces) drained
  pimientos

2 sliced medium onions
3 cloves garlic, crushed
1 tablespoon chopped parsley
1 teaspoon capers
Salt and pepper to taste

Remove stem from eggplant and cut in cubes. Sauté in oil for a few minutes. Add remaining ingredients. Stir occasionally. Cook for about 20 minutes.

Serves 4.

Frank Avruch

TV host and announcer

*F*rank Avruch has been with WCVB-TV (Channel 5), Boston, since it went on the air in 1972. He is host of the classic films series "The Great Entertainment" and co-host of "Sunday Open House," a community/public affairs program. A Boston native and graduate of B.U., Mr. Avruch lives in Newton, Massachusetts, with his wife, Betty, and sons, Matthew and Steven.

BRUNCH WITH FRANK AND JAN

"This was served on my 'Sunday Open House' program not too long ago and was received quite enthusiastically — over 250 requests for the recipe."

BANANA-ORANGE JUICE

Put 1 can (6 ounces) orange juice concentrate into blender container; add 3 cans cold water and 2 bananas, cut up; whirl until blended and serve.

Makes about 1 quart.

DUTCH BABIES WITH HAM

Combine 1 cup whipping cream, 8 teaspoons regular all-purpose flour, and ½ teaspoon salt. Beat in 8 eggs till well blended. Heavily butter three 8″ round cake pans and dust with flour. Arrange 1 cup diced cooked ham evenly between 3 pans, then divide the batter evenly between pans. (You can do this as much as an hour ahead; cover.) Bake in a very hot oven (450°) for 15-20 minutes, until edges are golden brown. Serve with hot Butter-Spiced Apples, powdered sugar, and lemon wedges.

Continued

Frank Avruch *continued*

BUTTER-SPICED APPLES

Peel, core, and thinly slice 4 large cooking apples. Melt 4 tablespoons butter in a large frying pan over medium heat. Add apples and turn with wooden spoon or spatula until apples are translucent. Mix 1 teaspoon cinnamon with ¼ cup granulated sugar. Sprinkle over apples — mix well. Serve hot.

FRANK AVRUCH'S 4-MINUTE PECAN PIE

"This is a quick and easy way to a delicious dessert — especially good for busy folks."

1 cup pecans	1 cup corn syrup
1 pie shell, unbaked	1 teaspoon vanilla
4 eggs	½ cup melted butter
½ cup sugar	

Place the pecans on the bottom of an unbaked pie shell. Combine remaining ingredients, adding one at a time and mixing each time you add an ingredient. Pour over pecans. Bake in oven at 350° for approximately 35 minutes, or until golden brown on top. (Place some aluminum foil around the edge of the pie crust to prevent the edges from turning too brown.)

Anne Baxter

Actress

A nne Baxter learned to cook while living in the bush of Australia and preparing six to seven meals a day — for her family, child's tutor, and frequent guests. "You can't be timid about cooking," she says, "don't tickle it, tackle it." An Academy Award winning actress, Ms. Baxter returned to the States to continue her acting career and spent many years on the West Coast, then moved east six years ago. "I've always loved Connecticut and have many friends here and elsewhere in the glorious New England area. After having been a resident 'alien' of seasonless California for 35 years, I finally made it back to beautifully unpredictable Connecticut and am savoring every moment."

SPINACH AND MUSHROOM SOUP

"This soup is excellent as a first course on holidays; or with cheese soufflé and a salad for luncheons."

1 box of Birds Eye spinach	2 egg yolks
1 pound of mushrooms	1 cup cream
¼ pound butter (1 bar)	Salt
2 cans of clear chicken broth	Pepper

Cook the spinach, following directions on the box. Drain well, but save juice. Run spinach through meat grinder (a messy performance). You should now have 1 cup of ground-up spinach and 1 cup of juice. Next stem mushrooms. Wash stems carefully, cover with 3 cups cold water and simmer until water is reduced by one half. Drain and save the juice. (Discard stems or chop and cook with caps.) Peel and chop the mushroom caps very fine, cook them slowly in 6 tablespoons of the butter for about 10 minutes, then add mushroom juice, spinach juice, and the chicken broth. Simmer gently about 15 minutes longer, then add half of the spinach if you like a thinnish soup, all of it if you like a hearty one. Simmer a while longer, then, when ready to serve, put the egg yolks in a soup tureen with cream, a little salt, and plenty of freshly ground black pepper, and beat until mixed; then stir in gradually the boiling hot soup. Add a small lump of butter, stir until melted,

Continued

Anne Baxter *continued*

and serve at once. Accompany with buttered, curried toast, made by
dipping both sides of trimmed slices of bread in melted butter, flavored with
curry powder. Lay on a cookie sheet and place in moderately hot oven until
golden brown. Serve hot.   *Serves 6-8.*

EASY AS PIE

"Sprinkle an unbaked pie shell with nutmeg and bake. During baking
of the shell prepare any fresh, sugared berries, or a mixture of several
(strawberries, pitted cherries, raspberries, etc.), and a bowl of unsweetened
whipped cream. Just pile berries in baked shell and top with whipped cream
at the last minute and you have a delightful summer dessert."

GINGER PEACHY

"Take six or seven ripe peaches, juice of one good-sized lime, three or four
heaping tablespoons light brown sugar, and some crystallized ginger. Mix all,
fill a baked pie shell, and top with unsweetened whipped cream. The
peaches do not darken because of the lime juice. Truly *delightful!*"

BROWNIES

*"These are as simple as one, two, three, and are among the first recipes I
taught my daughters."*

½ cup melted butter (oleo may be used)	2 eggs, beaten
	½ cup flour
2 squares chocolate, shaved, or an equivalent amount of cocoa	1 cup chopped walnuts
	¼ teaspoon salt
1 cup sugar	1 teaspoon vanilla

Melt butter in large saucepan, add shaved chocolate or cocoa, and keep
stirring until well melted and blended. Add sugar, beaten eggs, flour,
walnuts, salt, and vanilla. Stir well. Pour into a greased square tin. Bake for
25 minutes in a 350° oven. Dust with powdered sugar.

Orson Bean

Actor and comedian

"I was born in Burlington, Vermont, grew up in Cambridge, Massachusetts, and summered at my grandfather's place in Hartland, Vermont. My grandfather spent his whole life in Vermont. He used to warn me against southerners. 'Stay away from Hartford,' he'd say."

NEW ENGLAND RED FLANNEL HASH

"This is simply corned beef hash with diced beets mixed in. Both the taste and look of the hash are wonderfully changed by the addition of the beets."

Anne Bernays

Novelist

*A*nne Bernays is the author of seven novels, the latest being *The Address Book*. In addition to her writing, she teaches a fiction workshop in The Harvard Extension Program.

"My husband [Justin Kaplan] and children and I moved from New York City to Cambridge in 1959; we are still in the same house. We also have a summer place in Truro, on the Cape, where we live from June until mid-September."

JANE KENYON'S FRENCH BREAD

"Jane is the wife of poet Donald Hall and a fine poet herself. They live in Danbury, New Hampshire, in an old house owned by Don's grandfather. We have spent several weekends with them in this house talking for hours, playing Ping-Pong, and eating like crazy. For me, the peak of the meal is Jane's incredible bread which she claimed was so easy to make she was almost ashamed to give me the recipe. She's right. No baker, I can turn out two perfect loaves of the stuff in less than a morning, start to finish. It's better than any bread I've ever eaten. As you will see from the contents, it has no fat in it. Which is a trap because I always eat too much of it. I'm not sure, but I think she invented it herself, from fooling around with various recipes, none of which was quite good enough."

1 tablespoon sugar	5 cups flour (approximately)
2 cups warm water	2 teaspoons salt
1 tablespoon yeast	

Mix the sugar into the warm water and add yeast. Add 2½ cups of flour and salt and mix. Add enough flour to handle (approximately 2-2½ cups) and knead until smooth (2-3 minutes). Let rise about 40 minutes or until doubled. Divide in two and put in loaf pans (long French bread pans are best). Let rise about 40 minutes. Bake in preheated oven, 400°-425°, for 20-25 minutes. The crust on this bread is rich and very crunchy.

Leonard Bernstein

Conductor, pianist, and composer

*L*aureate conductor of the New York Philharmonic, Leonard Bernstein was born in Lawrence, Massachusetts, and attended Boston Latin School and Harvard. He studied conducting with Fritz Reiner and Serge Koussevitsky and piano with Helen Coates, Heinrich Gebhard, and Isabella Vengerova. Over the years he has frequently returned to the New England region: as assistant to Koussevitsky at the Berkshire Music Center and as a faculty member there; as professor of music at Brandeis; Charles Eliot Norton Professor of Poetry at Harvard; and lecturer at Harvard, with the television series "The Unanswered Question: Six Talks at Harvard." Mr. Bernstein resides in New York City.

LEMON MOUSSE

4 eggs
Pinch of salt
¾ cup sugar
1 tablespoon (1 package) Knox gelatin
3 tablespoons cold water

3 lemons, squeezed (6 tablespoons juice)
Grated rind of 2 lemons
½ cup sour cream, stirred until smooth
1 cup heavy cream, whipped

With a mixer, beat eggs and salt until light and foamy. Add sugar and continue to beat until *very* thick and fluffy. (You can continue beating while you prepare the gelatin.) Soften gelatin in the cold water; heat until gelatin dissolves. Add lemon juice and rind. (*Note:* Make sure gelatin is still dissolved; if not, place mixture back on heat, dissolve again, and then cool.) Stir gelatin mixture gently into eggs. Fold sour cream into whipped heavy cream, then fold into lemon mixture. Pour into serving bowl or into individual bowls, and chill for several hours. Top with whipped cream. It can be made a day ahead.   *Serves 8-10.*

James Bolle

Composer and conductor

James Bolle is founder and director of Monadnock Music, begun in 1966 in Nelson, New Hampshire, and music director as well as one of the founders of the New Hampshire Symphony Orchestra. He studied at Harvard, Aspen, Antioch, and Northwestern and was a composition student of Darius Milhaud.

"My wife is a native of Keene, New Hampshire, and I have lived in the region as a year-round resident since 1968. For a number of years before that we visited in the summer."

MOUCLADES D'ESNANDES

"A great mussel main dish."

¼ pint dry white wine
4 pints mussels, scrubbed and debearded
3 tablespoons butter
2 large cloves garlic, minced
6 ounces finely chopped shallot or mild onion

1 tablespoon flour
1½ cups milk
1 tablespoon anise seed
Salt and pepper
2 egg yolks
1½ tablespoons heavy cream

Use the wine to steam open the mussels. Remove and discard one shell of each mussel. Melt butter and cook garlic and shallot gently in it about 20 minutes. Stir in flour, liquid strained from the mussels, milk, and anise seed. Season with salt and pepper and boil it down a little. Beat egg yolks with cream and add to sauce. Cook without boiling until sauce thickens. Put the hot mussels into a large soup tureen and pour the hot sauce over them.

BRAZILIAN FISH STEW

"A favorite recipe of Jocelyn's, my wife; this is a hearty main dish."

1 clove garlic, minced
2 tablespoons olive oil
1 small onion, minced
4 tomatoes, peeled, seeded, diced
  (canned may be used)
½ green pepper, seeded and diced
1 tablespoon minced parsley
1 bay leaf

3 green chili peppers, chopped
  (canned may be used)
6 slices scrod fillets
1 cup clam juice or fish fumet
½ lemon, juiced
Salt
Pepper
Tabasco sauce

Brown garlic in olive oil in deep skillet. Add onion, tomatoes, green pepper, parsley, bay leaf, and chili peppers. Simmer 10 minutes. Cut fish into pieces, and add, together with clam juice or fish fumet, lemon juice, salt, and pepper. Add ½ cup water, cover, and simmer ½ hour or until fish flakes. Remove bay leaf. Add Tabasco sauce to taste and more salt and pepper if necessary.

HOT LEMON PUDDING

"A recipe of my mother's that I often make myself."

Cream 2 tablespoons butter and 1 cup sugar, then add 2 egg yolks, and the juice and grated rind of 1 lemon. Stir in ⅓ cup flour and ½ teaspoon salt, then 1 cup milk. Last, add 2 stiffly beaten egg whites (fold them in). Place batter in a buttered casserole set in a pan of hot water and bake 45 minutes in a moderate oven (350°).

Robert Brustein

Author, actor, teacher, and critic

*F*ounding director of the Yale Repertory Theater and American Repertory Theater, Robert Brustein has been involved with the theater for over 35 years. He is artistic director of the American Repertory Theater, director of the Loeb Drama Center, professor of English at Harvard, drama critic for *The New Republic,* and author of eight books. During his boyhood, Mr. Brustein attended summer camp in Center Ossipee, New Hampshire, and later graduated from Amherst College in Massachusetts. A Cambridge resident, he spends summers on Martha's Vineyard.

MAX BRUSTEIN'S TRADITIONAL SCRAMBLED EGGS

"Break required number of eggs into a bowl. Add pinch of salt, pepper, and dill. Stir with a fork. Brown ample amount of butter in frying pan. Add eggs, moving them from side to side with a spatula, so that they remain wet and juicy. Slide onto plate. Eat."

ROBERT BRUSTEIN'S SEDUCTION DINNER

Vichyssoise served with garlic bread
Pan-fried filet mignon with artichoke
Lettuce, tomato, and onion salad, with oil, vinegar, and dill dressing
Sara Lee cake with coffee
Generous helpings (before dinner) of very dry Stolichnaya martinis
VSOP Cognac after dinner
Soft music, dim lights, sweet talk

Art Buchwald

Columnist and author

Humorist Art Buchwald and his wife, Ann, have been spending summers in Vineyard Haven on Martha's Vineyard for the last 20 years. Known throughout the world for his syndicated column, which appears in more than 550 newspapers, Mr. Buchwald also has 25 books to his credit: one is a novel, two are guides to Paris, two are children's books, and the rest are collections of his columns and other writings. In 1982 he received the Pulitzer Prize for Outstanding Commentary. The Buchwalds have three children and live in Washington, D.C.

OUR FAMILY'S FAVORITE CHEESE CAKE/PIE

"Created by Ann's mother years ago."

Let 12 ounces of cream cheese soften while making the pie shell: Melt ¾ stick of butter and mix it with 16 graham crackers, ground up (or you can use about 2 cups graham cracker crumbs), line pie plate, and *chill*.

Mix the softened cream cheese, which should be beaten by electric beater or by hand until very creamy, with ½ cup granulated sugar and two eggs. Put cream cheese mixture into chilled pie shell and bake 20 minutes in a 350° oven.

Then remove from oven and pour on the top of the pie: ¼ cup granulated sugar mixed with ½ pint sour cream and 1 teaspoon vanilla. Then put back in oven and bake 5 minutes more.

Chill until ready to serve. Place strawberries, cut in half, around edge of pie if you want to be fancy.

Continued

Art Buchwald *continued*

THE BUCHWALD BAKED POTATO À LA CAVIAR

"The first thing I do is go out and buy the best caviar I can afford, but I don't stint because I never know when I'll eat caviar again. Take the caviar home and put it in the icebox, then place one large baked potato in the oven. If you plan to share the caviar with someone else, allow one baked potato for each person. After the potato is baked, take it out of the oven and slice one quarter off the top, then scoop out the white part of the potato leaving the skin intact. Whip the white part up with a little milk until it gets nice and creamy, then put it back into the skin. Make a little hole in the center, then take the caviar out of the icebox, open it carefully and put as much as you want to into the hole. Then take a dab of sour cream and put it on top of the caviar and sprinkle a few chives on the sour cream. Pour a shot of vodka and proceed to eat. This dish is especially good when you're tired and don't want to prepare a full meal. You can eat it every day and never get tired of it. It has a lot of protein and vitamins in it, and doctors recommend it."

William F. Buckley, Jr.

Author, editor, and lecturer

*E*ditor-in-chief of the *National Review,* which he founded in 1955, William F. Buckley is also host of "Firing Line," a weekly interview program shown on public television, a syndicated columnist ("On the Right"), and author of a score of books — both fiction and nonfiction, including *Saving the Queen, Up from Liberalism,* and *Atlantic High.* Mr. Buckley was born in New York City, grew up on the family's estate in Sharon, Connecticut, graduated from Yale University, and currently resides in Stamford, Connecticut. He and his wife, Patricia, have a son, Christopher.

SUPPLY-SIDE FUDGE

". . . I cooked feverishly during two summers, age 14 and 15 . . . [and] made a considerable sum of money from my cooking — something on the order of $24 or $25 per summer. I produced a most delicious fudge which I sold via an old ladies' institution in Sharon, Connecticut, at 65¢ per pound (with nuts, 75¢). My father was so unkind as to point out, somewhere along the line, that the economic model after which I had fashioned my enterprise was unrealistic inasmuch as I used exclusively ingredients provided gratis by my father's kitchen. Anyway (for a double portion): 1½ cups of milk, 4 squares of Baker's chocolate, ½ pound of butter, 2 cups of sugar. Stir until you see what looks like discrete globlets. Test these by dripping, by teaspoon, a drop or two. If they come down fragmented, you must leave the mixture under boil. If they come down whole, you are ready to lift the mess off the stove. (On no account should you pass by stage two from inattention, because the effect of this is a granular fudge.) At this moment, you should add a teaspoon of salt and, a minute or two later, two to three teaspoons of vanilla extract. The point of waiting this long is that you must not allow the vanilla to evaporate. If you are living in the post-industrial revolution you may submit the whole to a blender, adding nuts or not, according to market demands, always assuming you are not a supply-sider: in which case you should add the nuts *malgré soi.* The beating should continue until the stuff is very nearly cool, and only then pour it into a plate."

(Reprinted with permission from National Review, *May 1, 1981.)*

Bill Cavness

Actor and singer

*B*orn in San Antonio, Texas, and educated at the University of Texas, Bill Cavness has been sole reader for the broadcast series "Reading Aloud" for the past 26 years. The program is heard four nights a week on WGBH (Boston), WFCR (Amherst), and on other radio stations scattered across the United States. Mr. Cavness started working at WGBH in Boston in 1956 as senior producer for radio, a position he still holds. Recently, he was symposium speaker for the Center for the Book, at the Library of Congress.

CORN PUDDING A LA PUERTA DE AGUA DULCE

"This recipe came to me from my mother, who was born and raised on the headquarters division (La Puerta) of the vast King Ranch in Southeast Texas — once the largest private landholding in the world. For Texan friends, I often substitute for the bell peppers a very slightly smaller amount of chopped jalapeño, which is a shade warm for some Yankee tastes. For myself, I like it both ways. Makes a nice crusty-top, rich-tasting custard to go with a hearty entrée."

2 cups whole corn (drained if canned or thawed at room temperature if frozen)
2 tablespoons flour
4 tablespoons melted butter
2 tablespoons chopped pepper (red and/or green bell)
1 tablespoon chopped onion
1 egg, lightly beaten
¾ cup milk
Salt and pepper to taste
Grated cheese (Parmesan, Romano, or other)

Toss corn lightly in flour; add all but last ingredient and pour into greased baking dish. Set dish in a pan of water and bake for 45 minutes at 350°. To hold, allow to cool, cover and refrigerate. Reheat, again with dish in a pan of water, oven at 350°.

A few minutes before serving, sprinkle top with grated cheese, and run briefly under broiler.

Joyce Chen

Chef and businesswoman

Joyce Chen learned to cook when she was 16 and living in Shanghai. After moving to the Boston area in 1949, her culinary craft became her career. It began with her giving lessons in Chinese cooking — first to friends, then to adult education classes, and later on TV; then it expanded into a full-time business with the opening of her first Joyce Chen Restaurant, located in Cambridge, followed by the publication of a cookbook (recently updated). Today Mrs. Chen owns two Joyce Chen Restaurants and a Chinese grocery and gift shop, and markets a line of Chinese cookware and food products.

MINUTE SCALLION PANCAKES

"This is an ideal 'quick' snack or breakfast. Very easy to prepare and can be ready within minutes; delicious, too. All the ingredients are easily stored and obtainable. Scallion may be substituted with minced onion. In China we have a vegetable which has a distinct flavor between scallion and garlic, it is commonly used in this dish. Since I came to this country I substituted it with scallion, and added bacon or dried shrimp for more flavor. This is a wonderful way to use the white part of scallion for your salad and the green part for your pancakes."

1 egg	¼ teaspoon salt
⅔ cup flour	½ cup canned chicken broth, or
⅓ cup scallion — minced, about	water with ¼ teaspoon
2 stalks	monosodium glutamate (if
1 strip bacon — minced — or 1	desired) and ¼ teaspoon salt
heaping tablespoon dried	4 teaspoons cooking oil
shrimp, minced	

Mix the above ingredients (except oil) in a bowl into a thin paste (about 1 cup). Put 2 teaspoons oil in hot flat skillet over medium heat. Cover the bottom of the skillet evenly by tipping pan or use spatula. Pour half of the mixture from the bowl into skillet, spread out flat and cover the bottom

Continued

Joyce Chen *continued*

with the mixture. Cook until the edges are lightly browned, then turn to brown the other side. Using the remaining 2 teaspoons oil, cook the rest of the mixture in the same manner. Serve hot.

Makes two 8″-10″ round pancakes.

SWEET AND SOUR BEEF BALLS

"These are excellent as hors d'oeuvres at parties. The water chestnuts give the beef balls a good texture and the ginger root adds a delightfully light fragrance."

1 pound ground beef (extra lean)
⅛ teaspoon black pepper
1 tablespoon dry sherry
1 teaspoon salt
1 tablespoon soy sauce
2 tablespoons (level) cornstarch
1 tablespoon ginger root — minced (if available)

½ cup water chestnuts — minced. Canned or fresh, about 10 pieces or ½ cup (if available)
3 to 4 cups cooking oil (for deep frying)
Sweet and Sour Sauce (recipe follows)

1. Mix ground beef with black pepper, sherry, salt, soy sauce, cornstarch, ginger root, and water chestnuts. Be sure water chestnuts are finely minced so that ground beef will still form neat, round balls.

2. Take a heaping teaspoonful of ground beef mixture and roll into round balls about 1″-1½″ diameter. Place on a greased cookie sheet. Continue to make other balls in the same manner until you have used up all of the beef. You will have about 50 beef balls. Smaller beef balls are fine for cocktail parties.

3. Heat oil in wok to 350° over medium heat. Be sure to use enough oil so the beef balls are immersed and can brown evenly. Carefully slip the beef balls into the hot oil — about 10 to 15 balls at one time, depending upon the size of your pan. The balls should not be too crowded. When balls have evenly browned (about 3 minutes) remove to strainer and drain off oil. (You may do this step ahead of time. When ready to use, reheat cold beef balls in preheated 350° oven for about 5 minutes.) Prepare sauce.

SWEET AND SOUR SAUCE

⅓ cup cider vinegar
⅓ cup sugar
2 tablespoons (level) cornstarch

3 tablespoons soy sauce
⅓ cup water
¼ cup sesame seed (if desired)

Mix vinegar, sugar, cornstarch, soy sauce, and water together in a wok over medium heat. Stir continuously until mixture thickens. Add cooked beef balls and mix lightly until they are evenly coated. You may add ¼ cup sesame seeds if desired and stir lightly to coat. Serve hot, pierced with toothpicks, as hors d'oeuvres.

SPINACH — CHINESE STYLE

"This spinach goes well with Shanghai duck, Shanghai ham, or other dishes cooked with a large amount of soy sauce. Serve separately or put it around or under any one of these meat dishes. Drain if too watery.

"In China we have only the loose spinach in the market. We are all fond of the sweet taste of fresh spinach in late fall, especially with the pink root. We scrape the root with the fingernail and leave about ½-inch attached to the spinach stalk. The pink root with the green stalk leaves is so pretty. Poets describe this as the red-mouthed green parrot. Sometimes I go especially with my children to a nearby farm and get the owner's permission to dig the spinach this way.

"Beet tops and mustard greens can be cooked in the same way. They just need a little longer cooking, about 5 minutes, and add a little water, 3 to 4 tablespoons, when the liquid of vegetables is dried out while cooking."

1 ten-ounce package fresh spinach
  or 1 pound loose fresh spinach
2 tablespoons cooking oil

½ teaspoon salt
1 teaspoon sugar

Wash spinach thoroughly, even if packed, and drain well. Put oil and salt in a hot wok over a high heat. Add spinach first, then sugar. Stir and cook for about 1 to 2 minutes until the spinach is well wilted. Spread flat on a plate and serve hot.

Continued

Joyce Chen *continued*

PEKING MEAT SAUCE NOODLES

"This is the most well-known noodle dish from Peking. The best noodles to serve in this dish are pulled and stretched by hand from a very stiff and elastic dough. This kind of noodle is very smooth and chewy. The spaghetti here is closest to it. I compare Peking Meat Sauce Noodles to Italian spaghetti with meat sauce. I feel strongly that Marco Polo brought this recipe home from China in the thirteenth century. It is an old, good dish and widely beloved by Chinese, Japanese, and Koreans because the process of making it is easy and economical. Sometimes I serve this dish to a gathering of as many as two hundred Chinese friends."

1 bunch radishes — shredded with skin, about 1 cup
½ cucumber — shredded, peeled, seeded, about 1 cup
1½ cups raw bean sprouts — parboiled and drained
Half of a 10-ounce package spinach — parboiled (Squeeze out water and cut into fine pieces about ½″ long.)
1 cup ground pork
1 teaspoon dry sherry

⅔ cup bean paste*
1 tablespoon Hoi Sin sauce
2 tablespoons soy sauce
¼ teaspoon monosodium glutamate — optional
1 pound package spaghetti, thin or regular
1 tablespoon cooking oil
½ cup minced scallion
3 or 4 cloves garlic — skinned and minced

Prepare the vegetables as specified above. Mix pork with sherry and set aside. Mix the bean paste, Hoi Sin sauce, soy sauce, and monosodium glutamate together in a small bowl.

Cook the spaghetti in a large pot with at least 10 cups of boiling water. Stir the spaghetti in the water and bring to a boil. Cook over a low heat for 10 minutes (stir occasionally from bottom). Cook without cover or leave the cover open a little as the liquid will overflow if it is tightly covered. After it is cooked, cover the pot and let stay for 5 minutes. Rinse the cooked spaghetti (about 10 cups) in colander with hot water. Drain and serve hot with the sauce and vegetables.

While the spaghetti is cooking, cook the sauce: Put the oil in a wok over medium heat. Stir in the ground pork for 1 minute and then the minced scallions. Cook for another 1 minute. Add the bean paste mixture and after a few stirrings add ⅔ cup water and cook over *low* heat for less than 2 minutes, making a thin sauce.

Mix the spaghetti with sauce (about ¼ cup sauce to 1½ cups spaghetti) and vegetables (about 1 tablespoon each kind), and ¼ teaspoon garlic (if desired). Serve in a deep plate or individual bowls. Usually people eat more of this kind of noodles, about 1½ to 3 cups cooked spaghetti for one serving. If you are serving to a smaller party, then reduce the amount to half or as you need.

* Bean paste — There are two kinds of beans that make paste: fava beans and soy beans. Fava bean is sweeter, and soy bean paste is more salty. In this country they are both imported from Hong Kong and Japan. The bean paste which comes from Hong Kong is in two forms: Bean Sauce — bean paste with halves of soy bean (yellow bean); Ground Bean Sauce — bean paste in smoother form. This recipe uses ground bean paste. Sometimes it is not available in 1-pound cans, then you have to mash the beans into a smooth paste. (A 5-pound can is too much for you to use at home.) I prefer to use Japanese-made bean paste called Miso, which is shipped from Japan in wooden drums and does not have a metal smell. There are two varieties of Miso, white and dark. I mix them half and half. You can keep bean paste in a jar in the refrigerator for months.

(Recipes reprinted from Joyce Chen Cook Book *by permission of the author. Published by Joyce Chen Gourmet Products, Waltham, Massachusetts. Copyright 1962, 1983 by Joyce Chen. All rights reserved.)*

John Cole

Writer, editor, and teacher

John Cole (Yale '48) began his newspaper career in Maine over 25 years ago. He was editor of the *Bath-Brunswick Times-Record, Brunswick Record, Kennebunk Star,* and then the *Maine Times,* a statewide, weekly journal of opinion, which he co-founded. Mr. Cole has written for newspapers and magazines across the country, including *The Atlantic Monthly, Boston Globe, Washington Post, Yankee, Smithsonian,* and *Audubon,* and is author of *In Maine, From the Ground Up, CitySide-Countryside,* and other books. Currently contributing editor to *Maine Times,* correspondent for *Time* magazine, and a member of the boards of directors of several organizations and institutions, he is at work on his eighth book — a novel.

SEVEN-LAYER MOCHA CAKE

"Seven-Layer Mocha Cake, unless you happen to be close friends with an excellent cook, is a dessert served only in restaurants, and the good ones at that. I used to order it when my grandparents took me out to dinner as a boy in New York City. It became my idea of the perfect, indulgent dessert.

"Imagine how blessed I became when I learned that my wife, Jean, considered baking such cakes a rather routine challenge. She does the miracle as richly as any restaurant. However, I still use the privilege sparingly: birthdays, holidays, and other special occasions. Come to think of it, I haven't had any mocha cake for some time now.

"As for its health benefits, the cake hasn't one redeeming feature, which is another reason why it's my favorite."

6 eggs, separated	¼ cup cornstarch
1¼ cups sugar	½ teaspoon salt
2 tablespoons lemon juice	Mocha Cream Frosting (see
¾ cup sifted flour	below)

Beat egg yolks until thick and lemon-colored. Add sugar gradually, beating constantly with rotary beater (or electric beater), and 1 tablespoon lemon juice. Then sift in dry ingredients alternately with remaining lemon juice, beating until smooth. Fold in stiffly beaten egg whites. Spread a few tablespoonfuls of batter in each of two or three round 8-inch layer pans, 1 inch deep, lined on the bottom with waxed paper, then greased. Bake in a very hot oven (450°) for about 5 minutes or until lightly browned. Remove and cool. Repeat baking process until all the batter is used and 7 layers are baked. Spread with choice of frosting between layers and tops and sides of cake.

MOCHA CREAM FROSTING

⅔ cup granulated sugar
⅓ cup water
2 egg yolks
1 cup soft butter

1½ squares (ounces) unsweetened chocolate, melted
1 tablespoon very strong coffee
1½ tablespoons rum

Boil together the sugar and water to 240° (syrup forms a soft ball in cold water). Beat the egg yolks until fluffy. Add the syrup gradually, while beating, and continue beating until the mixture is cool. Add the butter bit by bit, until it has all been beaten in. Beat in the chocolate, coffee, and rum.

Abbott Lowell Cummings

Writer, lecturer, and teacher

After 28 years as executive director of the Society for the Preservation of New England Antiquities, Abbott Cummings resigned in order to accept a teaching position at Yale University. He is now first incumbent of the Charles F. Montgomery Professorship in American Decorative Arts. Writer and lecturer in the field of architectural history, Mr. Cummings has been adjunct professor at Boston University in the American and New England Studies Program since 1968. Born in St. Albans, Vermont (his mother's native town), Mr. Cummings grew up in Bennington and spent summers in Southington, Connecticut (his father's hometown). A resident of Boston from 1955 to 1983, he now lives in New Haven, Connecticut.

GRANDMA STOW'S PIE

"The following is not so much a recipe as a somewhat unusual way of preparing one of New England's oldest and most traditional dishes, the apple pie. It was always known in our family as 'Grandma Stow's' pie for my great-grandmother, Sarah (Walkely) Stow (1821-1904) of Southington, Connecticut. I have no way of knowing whether it was original with her or a way of making apple pie that was more widely current in Connecticut during her youth."

"In three ways this recipe differs from traditional methods:
(1) Ingredients — These should be *tart* apples. In fact, a doggerel expression of my great-grandmother's was often quoted in the family during my childhood: — 'A green apple pie by the Fourth of July.'
(2) Preparation — When the apples are cut up and placed in the pie plate with its bottom crust, the pie should be put into the oven to bake without any seasoning whatsoever. The top crust, moreover, should not be sealed, but laid gently over the pie with the edges floured to prevent sticking to the rim of the bottom crust.
(3) Seasoning — When the pie is baked (just before dinner so that it can be served warm as dessert) lift off the top crust with two long spatulas and add the following seasoning:

1 cup granulated sugar	Nutmeg (no more than ¼
1 tablespoon butter	teaspoon)
1 teaspoon vanilla	

Replace crust and allow seasoning to melt and flavor the whole pie."

Mary Cunningham

Business executive

A graduate of Wellesley College and Harvard Business School, Mary Cunningham is co-founder of Semper Corporation, a venture-capital firm that she runs with her husband William Agee. Earlier career work includes a position as vice president of strategic planning and project development of Joseph E. Seagram and Sons, Inc., and executive vice president for The Seagram Wine Companies; vice president of strategic planning at The Bendix Corporation; and assistant treasurer at The Chase Manhattan Bank. Ms. Cunningham, who serves on the boards of a variety of organizations and institutions, was recently voted by the *World Almanac* one of "The 25 Most Influential Women in America." A former international Alpine ski racer, she was born in Portland, Maine, raised in Hanover, New Hampshire, and currently resides in Oyster Harbors, Massachusetts.

DELICIOUS APPLE CRISP

4 to 6 medium apples	½ cup flour
¾ cup rolled oats	1 teaspoon cinnamon
¾ cup brown sugar	½ cup butter

Pare and core apples and slice thin. Arrange slices in a greased baking dish. Combine dry ingredients and mix well. Cut in butter. Sprinkle this mixture over the apples. Bake in a moderate oven, 350°, for 35-40 minutes. Serve warm and with vanilla ice cream.

*Clockwise from top: Peter De Vries, Mike Eruzione,
Larry Glick, Tammy Grimes*

Ron Della Chiesa

Radio host

Ron Della Chiesa has been host of WGBH radio's "MUSIC-AMERICA" program for seven years. Before that he had worked for Boston stations WBUR, WBOS, and WBCN. Raised in Quincy, Massachusetts, Ron began his long association with public broadcasting in 1960, starting at WGBH–TV 2 doing news and on-air booth work; he switched to WGBH radio full-time in 1969. On his afternoon program, heard Monday through Friday from noon to 5 P.M., Ron plays music from the big band era, Hollywood musicals, and Broadway shows, and works in some old-time radio nostalgia as well.

RISOTTO WITH SEAFOOD

2 cups rice
1 tablespoon olive oil
3½ cups chicken stock
1 (or more) garlic cloves, minced
1 small can tomato paste or 1 can
    marinara sauce

2 tomatoes, peeled and chopped
½ pound calamari
½ pound shrimp
1 dozen mussels or clams in shells
Parsley

Coat rice in hot oil and add half the chicken stock, garlic, tomato paste, and chopped tomatoes, and let simmer slowly, adding more liquid as needed. Add all the seafood and parsley, cover, and cook for 10 minutes until shells open. Do not overcook rice.

GNOCCHI WITH FRESH TOMATOES AND BACON

½ pound bacon
1 (or more) garlic cloves, finely
    chopped
1 onion, finely chopped
4 large ripe tomatoes, peeled and
    chopped

Chopped parsley
Parmesan or Romano cheese
1½ pounds boiled gnocchi,
    drained

Brown bacon and drain off grease. Sauté garlic and onion, add tomatoes, and cook a few minutes. Add parsley and cheese. Toss with gnocchi that has been well drained.

Tomie dePaola

Illustrator and author

Connecticut-born Tomie dePaola is illustrator of more than 120 children's books—and author of 41 of them. "I fell in love with upper New England as a young child when the family vacationed on Lake Champlain. I lived in Weston, Vermont, from 1956-1961, moved away — eventually to San Francisco — and in 1972 moved back to New England to teach at Colby-Sawyer College in New London, New Hampshire. Then taught at New England College in Henniker. Upper New England provides just the right atmosphere for me to do my children's books: the right combination of solitude, living with the seasons, and the small-town ambience, as well as big old houses with LOADS OF ROOM."

FLOSSIE'S CHRISTMAS EGGNOG

"I love to cook, love the holidays, so have chosen two extra-special family recipes. This one is for Flossie's Eggnog. My mother, Flossie, made it every Christmas. She and my dad had 'Open House' every Christmas Eve and it was terrific — the house would be full of neighbors and friends until the small hours of the morning. We kids loved it. We would hang over the banister to peek at all the festivities. The highlight would be my mom's eggnog — I still love it."

12 eggs	Brandy
½ cup sugar	Rye whiskey, bourbon, or blend
2 quarts whole milk	1 pint heavy cream
Crème de cacao	Nutmeg

Separate eggs. Whip yolks, add ½ cup sugar to yolks, and stir until dissolved. Then add milk. Add (according to taste): 2 or 3 jiggers of crème de cacao, 2 or 3 jiggers of brandy, and ½ to 1 cup of whiskey.

Whip egg whites until stiff and add to milk-egg mixture, beating slowly.

Whip heavy cream until stiff and add to milk-egg mixture, beating slowly. (I use an electric hand mixer at very low speed.) Taste and add more milk if too strong or add more whiskey if too weak. Chill for at least 1 hour so

Continued

Tomie dePaola *continued*

flavors "ripen." Top with fresh grated nutmeg and serve in eggnog cups with additional fresh nutmeg.

The same recipe can be made using vanilla extract instead of spirits — just add to taste.

NANA DEPAOLA'S EASTER BREAD

"This recipe is for my Italian grandmother's (Nana dePaola) Easter bread. She would braid the bread into "dolls," one for each of us. We always looked forward to the box arriving each Easter time. Of course, we weren't allowed to touch them until Easter Sunday. I used the bread dolls in a book about my Italian grandmother titled Watch Out for the Chicken Feet in Your Soup.*"*

6⅔ cups sifted unbleached flour	½ teaspoon sugar
1 cup sugar	7 eggs
1 teaspoon salt	Additional flour
1 teaspoon cinnamon	Vegetable oil
⅔ cup milk	1 egg yolk mixed with water for
10⅔ tablespoons shortening	glaze
1 package yeast	Uncooked eggs in shells for
½ cup warm water	"doll" faces

Mix dry ingredients (flour, 1 cup sugar, salt, cinnamon) together in a large *warmed* bowl or pan. Scald milk and add shortening; set aside to cool.

Dissolve yeast in warm water; sprinkle ½ teaspoon sugar on top and set aside in a warm place for about 10 minutes until mixture foams up. Slightly beat eggs. Make a "well" in the middle of the flour mixture; add milk with shortening, yeast, and eggs. Mix thoroughly, adding more flour if mixture is too sticky. Turn out on floured board and knead well (for about 10 minutes) until smooth and elastic.

Place in oiled bowl and brush oil on top (lightly); cover with plastic wrap and towels and set aside in warm draft-free place to rise. Let rise until double in bulk (this can take as long as 2-2½ hours).

Punch down and knead slightly (at this point it is possible to let the dough rise a second time if "lighter" bread is desired — be sure to knead after second rising). Let dough rest for 5 minutes covered so it does not dry out. Divide into pieces to braid into "dolls" or "circles" (see sketch); form them on a floured baking sheet. Cover with floured plastic wrap and towels and put in warm draft-free place to rise until nearly double in size (about 45 minutes to 1 hour). Preheat oven to 375°. Brush with egg glaze mixture and bake 40-45 minutes until golden brown and bread sounds slightly "hollow" when tapped. Cool on wire racks.

"DOLLS"

Recipe will make 4 small dolls. Divide dough into six equal pieces. Divide two pieces in half. You will end up with 4 large portions and 4 half portions. Each doll takes 1 large portion and 1 half portion. Roll out large portion with hands into a long rope (not too thin). Roll half portion so it is ½ the length of the long rope. Place as in sketch.

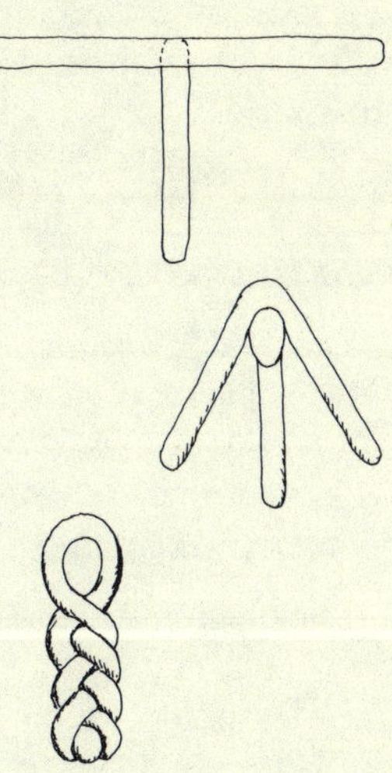

Put uncooked egg where "ropes" come together. The egg will be the "head" or "face" of the doll.

Braid in usual fashion. Braided "doll" will look something like this:

When making each doll, be sure to cover remaining dough so it will not dry out.

"CIRCLES"

Recipe will make 2 circles with 3 eggs. Divide dough into six equal pieces. Roll three pieces with hands into equal length ropes. Braid into a circle placing uncooked eggs equi-distant in the braid.

Resulting circle will look something like this:

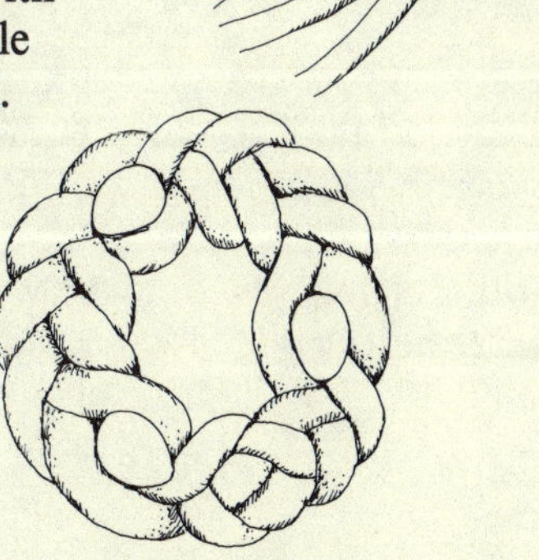

Carl de Suze

Correspondent, critic, and director

Carl de Suze was "born on a boat in New York Harbor as it bumped the pier." Educated at Bowdoin College, he has lived in Connecticut, Massachusetts, and Maine, where he began in radio in 1938 with station WGAM, Portland. From 1942 to 1982 he served as morning man and foreign correspondent for WBZ, Boston, and is currently correspondent and critic-at-large for the station as well as director of the Westinghouse Regional Affairs Council, which broadcasts week-long quarterly reports on major issues of both corporate and community interest.

CHICKEN BANGALORE

"This is a favorite of mine since (providing the ingredients are at hand) it makes for an elegant meal quickly when unexpected guests drop in. I picked it up in South India when I was doing a three-month report on Asia in 1957. It's been revised by me, and before that by my hostess, one of the film-maker Flaherty's daughters."

4 boned and skinned chicken breasts	2 tablespoons turmeric
4 teaspoons Dijon mustard	2 tablespoons coconut snow or flakes
Salt and pepper to taste (Indians use hot Nepal pepper)	½ cup orange juice
1 cup light cream	½ cup pineapple juice
1 large egg	¼ cup honey
1 teaspoon madras curry powder	Topping (toasted shredded coconut, bacon snips, raisins,
1 tablespoon coriander	and scallion or chive snips)

Rub chicken with mustard, salt, and pepper. Place in greased casserole. Blend cream, egg, curry, coriander, turmeric, coconut snow, orange and pineapple juice, and honey. Pour over chicken. Bake 30 minutes in 375° oven, basting occasionally. Serve on halved baking powder biscuits or rice with Topping. Accompany with mixed greens or spinach salad with sweet and sour dressing.

Serves 4.

Peter De Vries

Writer and editor

Peter De Vries was an editor of *Poetry* magazine when he left in 1944 to go to work for *The New Yorker*, with which he is still associated. Among his many works (over 20 novels) are *Reuben, Reuben*; *Slouching Towards Kalamazoo*; and *Consenting Adults*. Mr. De Vries and his wife, author/poet Katinka Loeser, have lived in Westport, Connecticut, since 1947.

MOULES REMOULADE

"The very words 'moules remoulade,' in their evocatively lush phonetics, make my mouth water, and even my eyes, with tears of happy anticipation."

"Buy a can of mussels, if you don't want to steam a mess yourself. For the sauce: 2 cups mayonnaise, 2 cloves garlic, finely chopped, 1 tablespoon finely chopped tarragon (or dill), 1 teaspoon dry mustard, 2 hard-cooked eggs, finely chopped, 1 tablespoon capers, 1 tablespoon finely chopped parsley, 1 teaspoon anchovy paste. Mix all ingredients thoroughly and let stand for 2 hours. Occasionally, by way of improvisation, I slip in a mustard other than the standard dry kind, one of the numerous prepared mustards available these days, often themselves sauces of a sort, and thus surprise even myself.

"Send a plate of this downhill with a bottle of Saint-Verain or Puligny-Montrachet and for an hour forget your troubles."

Robert F. Drinan, S.J.

Clergyman, lawyer, and former congressman

*B*orn in Boston, Father Drinan was the first Roman Catholic priest ever to serve as a voting member of Congress. Dean of Boston College Law School for a dozen years, he now resides in Washington, D.C., where he is a professor at Georgetown University Law Center. Father Drinan is the author of five books, the latest of which is *Beyond the Nuclear Freeze.*

Boston Baked Beans

1 pound dried navy or pea beans
   (about 2 cups)
½ pound salt pork (without rind)
1 medium onion, sliced
¼ cup brown sugar (packed)

3 tablespoons molasses
1 teaspoon salt
¼ teaspoon dry mustard
⅛ teaspoon pepper

Place beans in large saucepan and cover with water. Heat to boiling; boil 2 minutes. Remove from heat and let stand 1 hour. Add water, if necessary to cover beans; simmer uncovered 50 minutes or until tender. (Do not boil or beans will burst.) Drain beans, reserving liquid.

Heat oven to 300°. Cut salt pork into several pieces; layer with beans and onion in ungreased 2-quart bean pot or casserole. Stir together remaining ingredients and 1 cup of the reserved liquid; pour over beans. Add enough of the remaining reserved liquid (or water) to almost cover beans. Cover. Bake 3½-4 hours, removing cover for last half hour of baking time; if beans look dry during baking, stir. *Serves 6-8.*

Gingery Fruit Salad

2 cups sliced, peeled fresh
  peaches or nectarines
¼ cup sugar
1 teaspoon lemon juice
1 three-ounce package cream
  cheese, softened

½ teaspoon ground ginger
1-2 tablespoons milk
3 cups torn mixed salad greens
1 cup chilled fresh raspberries
½ cup chilled fresh blueberries

Place peach slices in bowl; toss with sugar and lemon juice. Cover and refrigerate about one hour. Drain peaches, reserving syrup. Cover peach slices and refrigerate. To prepare dressing, add cream cheese and ginger to reserved syrup; beat until smooth. Stir in milk till dressing is desired consistency. Chill.

Place salad greens in salad bowl. Arrange peach slices, raspberries, and blueberries atop greens. Serve with dressing. *Serves 6.*

Michael S. Dukakis

Governor of Massachusetts

*M*assachusetts Governor Michael Dukakis was born and raised in Brookline, where he still resides. Graduate of Swarthmore College and Harvard Law School, he entered the Massachusetts House of Representatives in 1963, served as governor of Massachusetts from 1975-79, was lecturer and director of Intergovernmental Studies at Harvard University's Kennedy School of Government from 1979-82, and in 1983 returned to the office of Massachusetts governor. He and his wife, Kitty, have three children.

CHICKEN CASSEROLE

"This is one of my family's favorites. It is very quick to prepare and always turns out perfectly."

8 boned chicken breasts	1 can cream of mushroom soup
1 pint sour cream	1 teaspoon tarragon

Place chicken in 13″ x 9″ casserole. Combine remaining ingredients, pour over chicken, and bake in 325° oven for approximately 1 hour, uncovered. Baste once or twice.

Serves 6-8, depending on the size of chicken breasts.

TOURLOU

"An old favorite, especially good in the summertime, with fresh New England vegetables!"

1 large eggplant (slender), cut up in large cubes

3 green peppers, cut in strips

2 or 3 large zucchini, cut in large pieces

3 large onions, thinly sliced

1 cup chopped parsley (Italian is best)

1 can whole tomatoes puréed in blender

½ small can tomato sauce

1 cup olive oil

Spread all but last ingredient in oiled pan (16″ x 12″). Pour olive oil over all. Add dash of salt and pepper. Bake at 350° till bubbly, 300° after. Stir every so often while baking. Should be fairly dry, not watery, when done. Serve hot or cold.

Harold E. Edgerton

Educator, electrical engineer, and inventor

*P*rofessor emeritus at the Massachusetts Institute of Technology, Harold (Doc) Edgerton left his home state of Nebraska in 1926 in order to attend M.I.T. — and he has been there ever since, first as a student, then as a professor. His involvement with stroboscopic photography and sonar equipment earned him a worldwide reputation, and today his scientific photographs are being appreciated in the art world, too. Galleries are exhibiting his work, and one of his most famous photographs (of a crown-shaped drop of milk after it hits a saucer) hangs in the Museum of Modern Art.

Both of the following recipes are from a collection of Doc Edgerton's mother, Mary (Mrs. Frank E.) Edgerton.

MRS. EDGERTON'S HOMEMADE BREAD

1 cake Fleischmann's yeast or 1 package Dry Red Star	2 cups warm water
	1 teaspoon salt
½ cup brown sugar	1 egg
½ cup Crisco	7 cups flour (about)

Dissolve yeast, brown sugar, and shortening in the warm water; add salt and slightly beaten egg, and mix well. Add enough sifted bread flour to handle easily, about 7 cups in all. (Mrs. Edgerton uses 1 cup whole wheat flour to each batch of bread, but says this is optional.)

Set dough in warm place, free from drafts, to rise. (She lets her bread dough rise in the oven, and in cold weather barely heats the oven.) Let dough rise until double in bulk, work down, and let rise again until light (double in bulk). Shape into loaves or rolls and put into greased pans. This makes two loaves and a small pan of rolls. Bake in a 400° oven until golden brown.

COWBOY STEAK

*"When I [Doc Edgerton's father] was out in Cherry County, Nebraska, near
Valentine, a cowboy told me that he could cook the best steak in the world.
This is the way he did it, and for many years, I often cooked the steak for a
dinner when we had house guests. It was usually the last dinner of their visit
here. I would go to the butcher's, pick out the steak, carry it home, with a
pound of butter. Then the whole family would stand around the stove while I
cooked the steak . . . When it was done, we would all rush to the table and
eat it while it was steaming hot. Then Mary would bring the gravy, and we
would eat it on bread. When this was done, then we would take some interest
in what else there was to eat.*

"Put a big skillet on the stove, and let it get hot, with about a stick of butter
in it, until the butter bubbles up. In the meantime, salt the steak well on
both sides; then dredge it in flour, 2 or 3 times on each side. Then slide it
into the hot fat in one big piece. Cover and let it get hot. Turn once, cover,
then again and again until each side has been on the heat twice, and is
nicely browned. Then rush to the table, and serve on hot plates, with steak
knives."

Mike Eruzione

Hockey player

ike Eruzione was the captain who led the 1980 United States Olympic Hockey Team to its Gold Medal victory. A native of Winthrop, Massachusetts, he was captain of the Boston University hockey team his senior year, finished as second leading scorer in B.U. history, and was cited as best defensive forward in the East all four years. After graduation Mike played with the Toledo Golddiggers of the International Hockey League and was voted the McKenzie Award Winner, which is annually presented to the most outstanding American-born hockey player in the league. Mike serves as a spokesperson for the New Balance Shoe Company, based in Boston, does charity work, public appearances, and promotional endorsements, and is associated with Robert Landau Associates and the Madison Square Garden Communication Network.

ZUCCHINI BREAD

2 cups Bisquick	3 eggs
1½ cups shredded zucchini	1 teaspoon vanilla
¾ cup sugar	3 teaspoons ground cinnamon
¼ cup vegetable oil	2 teaspoons ground nutmeg

Heat oven to 350°. Grease bread pan. Beat all ingredients on low speed, scraping bowl occasionally, for one minute. Pour into pan. Bake until done — 50-55 minutes. Cool 10 minutes. Remove from pan. Keep in refrigerator.

Carrot Cake

4 eggs
1½ cups Wesson oil
1½ cups sugar
3 cups shredded carrots
2 cups flour

2 teaspoons cinnamon
1 teaspoon soda
1 teaspoon salt
Dash of nutmeg
Dash of cloves

Beat eggs slightly and blend in all other ingredients. Bake in two round pans (greased and floured) at 350° for 45 minutes, or in a 13″ x 9″ Pyrex dish at 350° for one hour.

ICING

8 ounces cream cheese
1 stick butter

1 cup confectioners sugar
2 teaspoons vanilla

Mix icing ingredients and ice cooled cake. Keep in a cool place.

Bramwell Fletcher

Actor

*B*ramwell Fletcher was born in Yorkshire, England, and raised in London. As a young actor, he starred in London before moving to the United States to play a variety of roles in Hollywood and New York that ranged from the poet in Sean O'Casey's drama *Within the Gates* to Professor Higgins in *My Fair Lady.* During the 1960s, Mr. Fletcher toured the country from coast to coast with his one-man show as George Bernard Shaw. After settling in New Hampshire in 1970 when he and Lael Wertenbaker married, he took up painting, a lifelong passion, and later began writing his first book.

SHEPHERD'S PIE

"This is constructed rather than made and can be varied. It is baked in a greased casserole."

Bottom layer: ground meat, preferably lamb
2nd layer: onions and green peppers, chopped and sautéed in butter
3rd layer: ground carrots, lightly cooked or raw
4th layer: green peas, canned or fresh, lightly cooked
Top layer: mashed potatoes, heaped nicely and dotted with butter

Arlene Francis

Actress

Arlene Francis was born in Boston and educated in New York. During her career as an actress, she has performed on radio and television, in motion pictures, and on the stage. For 17 years she was a panelist on the television show "What's My Line?" Miss Francis and her husband, producer and actor Martin Gabel, live in New York City.

BROOKEFOREST EGGS

"The only way to understand or appreciate this dish is to eat it. It's unique. And served with grilled tomatoes or a fresh, green salad, it's unbeatable."

"Allow two eggs per person. Take a third of those eggs, break them into a mixing bowl, and beat lightly with a fork. Into an ungreased casserole pour enough of the beaten eggs to barely cover the bottom of the casserole. Sprinkle chopped, cooked ham over that. Then add chopped green pepper and sliced mushrooms. Salt and pepper liberally. Now comes the trick: Take three or four of the unbroken eggs, crack the shells and deposit the eggs, with the yolks unbroken, right on top of the other ingredients. Drop these eggs here and there at random, the number depending on how many you're using all together, but do be careful to keep the yolks intact. Next, cover the whole thing with slices of American cheese. (Use a sharper cheese if you prefer it tangy.) Now, start all over, building another layer. Cover that layer with cheese and build another — until the eggs are all used. If you're having a crowd, you can build five or six or even seven layers this way. Top it off with a layer of sliced cheese, sprinkle with paprika, and put it in a slow-to-medium oven (325° to 350°) for two hours. If it's a big casserole, make it two and one-half. If the guests are late, turn the oven to low and let it go. The way to test it is to stick a good-sized spoon into the middle. If the spoon stands up, it's done."

R. Buckminster Fuller

Engineer, inventor, mathematician, architect, philosopher, poet . . .

Buckminster Fuller was born in Milton, Massachusetts, in 1895 of a ninth-generation Massachusetts family, and for nearly 80 years was a summer resident of Bear Island, Maine. Recognized throughout the world as a design scientist, architect, author, poet, engineer, and educator, he was perhaps best known for his invention of the geodesic dome. During his long and industrious life he was awarded 48 honorary doctorates, served as visiting professor or lecturer at over 600 universities around the world, and received major architecture and design awards, including the gold medal of the American Institute of Architects. In addition, President Reagan presented him with the Medal of Freedom, the highest civilian honor in the United States. On July 1, 1983, Mr. Fuller died of a heart attack, just short of his 88th birthday.

CREAM OF TOMATO ICE CREAM

"I take fresh tomatoes and fresh rich cream and cook together a cornstarch and fresh egg custard. I pulverize and strain the tomatoes and put in a dash of salt and pepper and a few spoonfuls of sugar (to taste). I then add in the rich cream an equal amount of cornstarch egg custard. There should be equal quantities of each of the main ingredients — mix liquid tomato, rich cream, and liquid starch custard, say one quart of each, and then freeze in a regular old-fashioned wooden freezer with the churn, surrounded by chopped ice and rock salt. (It is to be served in lieu of hot soup on hot days, and served on a bed of chopped green peppers and watercress.)"

(Reprinted from SYNERGETIC STEW: Explorations in Dymaxion Dining, ©1982 Buckminster Fuller Institute, 3501 Market Street, Philadelphia, PA 19104.)

Larry Glick

Radio talk-show host

Born and raised in Roxbury, Massachusetts, Larry Glick has been in broadcasting for 30 years. His first job in radio was with WLNH in Laconia, New Hampshire; his next while in the Army, stationed in Germany. Some years later in 1968 he joined WBZ, Boston, where he has been ever since. In addition to his talk show, Larry's other passions are hypnosis (he conducts self-help programs for losing weight, stopping smoking, and reducing stress) and flying his Piper Warrior.

"On a trip to Ireland some years ago, I learned that 'Glick' is a Gaelic word meaning 'clever'. Following are three 'Glick' recipes that I'm sure you will enjoy."

BREAST OF CHICKEN LA DONNA

4 tablespoons cornstarch	4 tablespoons butter
1 teaspoon salt	2 Delicious apples, cored, sliced
⅛ teaspoon white pepper	1 ounce Benedictine liqueur
⅛ teaspoon freshly grated nutmeg	1 cup heavy cream
4 individual breasts of chicken, skinless, boneless	Watercress to garnish

Blend cornstarch with salt, pepper, and nutmeg. Wash and dry the breasts of chicken with paper towels. Draw each through the cornstarch mixture; shake off excess.

In a large frying pan, melt butter over medium heat. Slowly sauté chicken and apple slices in butter, turning often. Remove apple slices and keep warm while chicken cooks until done. Warm the Benedictine, light with a match, and pour flaming over the chicken. Tilt pan about. As flames die out, remove chicken to another pan and keep warm.

With a wire whip, stir pan drippings. Add the heavy cream. Continue to stir over medium heat, reducing cream to desired thickness, about 10 minutes. Taste and adjust seasoning.

Continued

Larry Glick *continued*

Arrange breasts of chicken on warmed serving dish, separating each with apple slices. Pour sauce over chicken. Garnish with watercress and serve at once.
Serves 4.

SHEPHERD'S PIE

"This recipe is very flexible. Amounts of meat, potatoes, and vegetables may be increased for hearty appetites."

Mashed potatoes (enough for 6 servings)
2 tablespoons parsley flakes
2 cups cubed lamb, beef, or veal
¼ cup chopped onion
2 cups cooked vegetables (peas, carrots, corn)
2 cups gravy

Heat oven to 350°. Prepare mashed potatoes — stir in parsley flakes; set aside. In large mixing bowl, stir together remaining ingredients. Divide meat mixture evenly among 6 individual baking dishes (ungreased). Mound potatoes on meat mixture. Bake uncovered 30 minutes or until potatoes brown slightly.
Serves 6.

IRISH BREAD, A GAELIC BLESSING

2½ cups flour
2 teaspoons baking powder
1 teaspoon salt
½ teaspoon baking soda
¼ cup butter or margarine
½ cup sugar
1 egg, beaten
1½ cups buttermilk
1 cup raisins
½ cup currants
1 tablespoon caraway seeds (optional)

Sift together flour, baking powder, salt, and soda, and set aside. Cream the butter and sugar. Add beaten egg and buttermilk; blend well. Add liquid mixture to dry ingredients; mix by hand only until dry ingredients are well moistened. Fold in raisins, currants, and caraway seeds. Pour into greased 1½-quart glass casserole. Brush top with melted butter or margarine; sprinkle with a little sugar. Bake at 375° for 30 minutes, then reduce to 325° for about 30 minutes longer. Test in the middle of the loaf before removing from oven (for easier toasting, using a long pan, 13″ x 4″ x 2″, works well, too).

Tammy Grimes

Actress, singer, and comedienne

"**I** was born in Lynn, Massachusetts, on January 30th, when my parents were on their way home to Boston from a party. My mom was 'very big' with the Charleston, and lost her head I guess, and also 'very big' with me. We lived in Boston, where my father managed 'us' and the Hotel Somerset, and then at 'The Country Club' in Chestnut Hill, Massachusetts, dining mostly on 'Pheasant Under Glass.' Summers were spent in a quiet village in southern New Hampshire.

"My father owns The Colonial Inn in Concord, Massachusetts, which was built in 1775. All the food prepared there is Yankee cooking. I remember Brown Bread and Baked Beans in a Big Brown Pot every Sunday — that's what we were brought up on. I live in New York City and although this 'madness captivates me here' everyone almost always asks, 'But where are you *from*?' I *proudly* say, 'I'm from Boston.' 'Oh!' they say, *surprised*. 'Yup,' I say. 'Once a Yankee, always a Yankee.' "

WOOL'S-GRIMES' ECSTATIC BROWNIES

"I have been baking these brownies for 15 years, and there has never *been a guest who didn't say: 'These are the most delicious I've ever tasted.' They were created in Long Island on a warm sunny day when Wool and Grimes decided to go 'straight to heaven' in the kitchen."*

1 teaspoon baking powder	5 squares Baker's unsweetened
2 cups sugar	chocolate
1 cup flour	½ pound butter (oh my!)
4 eggs	

Combine dry ingredients in a bowl and set aside. In separate bowl lightly whip the eggs. Melt chocolate and butter in double-boiler until smooth. Pour into first bowl with dry ingredients. Add eggs and stir. Pour into baking pan — standard size, 10 inches. Bake in oven preheated to 350°. Watch carefully after 30 minutes; it usually takes 40 to 45 minutes. The point is that they must be moist.

Continued

Tammy Grimes *continued*

Lemon Bars

1 cup plus 2 tablespoons softened
  butter
½ cup sifted confectioners sugar
¾ cup sifted bleached all-purpose
  flour

3 eggs
1 cup sugar
½ cup lemon juice

Spread a 9″ x 9″ baking pan with 2 tablespoons of the butter. Set aside.

Beat the remaining butter in a bowl with a whisk, or electric beater, until creamy. Gradually add the confectioners sugar — mixture should be fluffy when concluded. Add flour and stir with spoon till everything is smooth. Spread evenly in the bottom of the baking pan.

Beat eggs lightly in a bowl; gradually beat in the sugar and lemon juice. Spread evenly over the pastry. Bake at 350° in a preheated oven for 25 minutes.

Remove, cool, and cut into bars.

H-L

Clockwise from top: David Ives, Stephen King, Margaret Heckler, Frances Minturn Howard

Marvelous Marvin Hagler

Boxer

*M*arvelous Marvin, as he is known not only in the sports arena but also on legal documents, started training as a boxer at age 15 when he and his family moved to Brockton, Massachusetts. In 1980 he defeated Englishman Alan Minter to become the combined World Boxing Association and World Boxing Council middleweight champion. He has successfully defended his title nine times to date, amassing a professional record at 59-2-2. Marvelous Marvin's training camp is in Provincetown on Cape Cod; his home is in Hanover, Massachusetts, where he lives with his wife, Bertha, and their four children. When he isn't boxing or involved with other commitments, he tries to spend some of his free time pursuing his lifelong hobby of keeping and training pigeons.

The following recipes are favorites of Marvelous Marvin's as prepared by his mother, Mrs. Ida Mae Long.

OLD-FASHIONED STEW

3 pounds neck bones or stew beef
1 large can of tomato paste
½ cup ketchup
½ teaspoon Worcestershire sauce
Tabasco sauce (few drops)
½ to 1 cup red cooking wine
 (optional)
Salt and pepper to taste
6 (or more) white potatoes, diced
1 clove of garlic, minced

1 green pepper, diced
1 onion, diced
1 stalk of celery, diced
4 carrots, diced
1 bay leaf
1 large can whole kernel corn
1 large can tomatoes (whole or
 stewed)
½ package of okra, chopped
 (optional)

Cook the meat (neck bones an hour, stew beef half an hour) in a large pot with tomato paste, ketchup, Worcestershire sauce, Tabasco, wine, and salt and pepper. In another big pot (4 quarts or more) cook potatoes, garlic, green pepper, onion, celery, carrots, bay leaf, corn, tomatoes, and okra for 30 minutes. Then add to meat and cook for another 30 minutes. Let simmer until time to eat. Serve with crackers.

STUFFED BLUEFISH

6- to 8-pound bluefish, fileted and
  split
2 large onions
1 small green pepper

1 pound package bacon
1 lemon, sliced
Lemon juice
Melted butter (optional)

Put fish, skin side down, in a large pan and bake for 20 minutes at 350°.
Slice the onions and green pepper, reserving a few slices of each for garnish.
Cut up bacon and cook with onion and green pepper until bacon is done.
Place the vegetables, bacon, and lemon slices inside the fish. Put reserved
onion and green pepper slices on top of fish, sprinkle with lemon juice,
drizzle with butter, if desired, and bake for 20 more minutes. Before serving,
top with a couple of slices of lemon and sprinkle with paprika.

Serves 12-14.

BOILED LOBSTER

6 chicken lobsters
Bay leaf
Bay Seasoning (or seasoned salt)

2 corn on the cob
1 quart beer (any kind)
Butter to taste

Fill a 10-quart pot with water, bring to a boil, and add lobsters, bay leaf,
and Bay Seasoning. Cook, covered, for 10 minutes. Add corn and cook 5
minutes; then add beer, reduce heat, and cook slowly for 15 minutes. Add a
dollop of butter, stir until melted, and serve immediately.

Donald Hall

Poet and editor

Eight years ago Donald Hall quit teaching and moved with his wife, Jane, also a poet, to his ancestral home in New Hampshire, where he wanted to live full-time and work as a free-lance writer. "I was born in Connecticut and visited this house first when I was six weeks old. My mother and grandmother were born here. My great-grandfather settled here in 1865. The postal address is Danbury, the telephone exchange is Andover, and we pay taxes to the town of Wilmot." Some years ago Mr. Hall wrote a book about his memories of New Hampshire called *String too Short to be Saved* and in the summer of 1983, the Peterborough (N.H.) Players staged an adaptation of it under the title of *Ragged Mountain Elegies.* His latest book of poems is *Kicking the Leaves.*

New England Baked Dinner

"New England baked dinner uses the oven to cook four things at the same time: meatloaf, potatoes, onions, and mushrooms.

"For four people obviously you need four baking potatoes. Add four medium-sized onions, maybe half a pound of mushrooms, and meatloaf to suit the ambitions of the crowd. This recipe will serve four delicate meatloaf-eaters.

"Add to a pound and a half of hamburg a raw egg, a small can of tomato paste, or half a can if you want to limit the tomato flavor, a roughly chopped onion of medium size, a pinch of dry mustard, three pinches of basil, salt and pepper, a pinch of red pepper, three squished cloves of garlic, and twenty-four tiny-diced chunks of green pepper; add maybe four tablespoons of bread crumbs. Assemble by stirring violently. Bake for fifty minutes at 375°.

"Everybody knows how to bake potatoes.

"Baking onions is rarer and easier. You do not need to wash or scrape an onion. Usually I rub away the loosest skins. Onion juice *does* drip onto your pan, so I tend to bake them on a piece of foil set in the pan, in order to save scouring. Bake them at 375° for 50 minutes, and roll them out onto the dinner plate. Invite your guests to open them up like a baked potato, add butter and salt as they wish . . . For myself, I find that the hot onion, cooked in its own juice, needs no tarting up.

"Clean the mushrooms, wrap them in foil, and bake them as long as you wish. They do not require fifty minutes — probably fifteen would do — but they will not suffer unduly. Shake them out of the foil onto the plate, and pour the mushroom juice, self-generated by the baking, over the mushrooms.

"That's it."

Ernest Hebert

Writer

*E*rnest Hebert was born and raised in Keene, New Hampshire, where he still lives with his wife, Medora, and daughter, Lael. He is the author of *The Dogs of March* and *A Little More Than Kin,* novels about modern life in rural New England, and writes a weekly column for *The Boston Sunday Globe Magazine.*

FRIED RICE GLUTCH

"Fried Rice Glutch is my own fast food. It can be eaten cold or hot, and is especially valuable during fishing season when I am often taken by sudden urges to drop everything, drive up to Chapman Pond in Sullivan, New Hampshire, launch my canoe and wet a line.

"I cook a cup of brown rice, and fry it in a little butter with cut-up pork strips, or any leftover meat, an egg, an onion, a green pepper, a sprinkling of tamari sauce and tremendous amounts of garlic. One of my cooking rules is there's no such thing as too much garlic. The glutch lasts at least a week in the refrigerator. Whenever I need a quick meal, there it is. It can either be refried with leftover vegetables, or brought along in a plastic dish and eaten cold with a spoon from the canoe."

Margaret Heckler

Cabinet member and former congresswoman

argaret Heckler was born in Flushing, New York, and attended Albertus Magnus College in New Haven and Boston College Law School (where she was the only woman and sixth-ranking graduate in her class). She served 16 years in the U.S. House of Representatives from the 10th Congressional District in Massachusetts, and on January 12, 1983, was nominated by President Reagan to serve as Secretary of Health and Human Services. The following recipes are from the luncheon that followed the swearing-in ceremony.

VICHYSSOISE

4 medium leeks	2 cups cream
1 large onion	¼ teaspoon mace
2 tablespoons butter	¼ teaspoon salt
5 medium potatoes	¼ teaspoon white pepper
6 cups chicken stock	Chopped chives

Sauté minced leeks and onion for three minutes in butter. Slice potatoes very thin, add them to chicken stock along with leeks and onion, and simmer for 15 minutes or until tender. Process in blender, then add cream and seasonings and garnish with chives.

Continued

Margaret Heckler *continued*

VEAL AND MUSHROOMS WITH SHALLOT SAUCE

2½-pound leg of veal
¼ cup white wine
2 tablespoons lemon juice
2 cups flour
2 teaspoons salt

½ teaspoon pepper
⅛ teaspoon garlic powder
2 tablespoons Parmesan cheese
1 teaspoon paprika

Slice veal into strips one inch wide by four inches long. Pound veal on both sides with a mallet. Place veal strips in a pan and sprinkle each layer with white wine and lemon juice. Set aside. Combine flour, salt, pepper, garlic powder, Parmesan cheese, and paprika. Mix well. Coat the veal strips with the flour mixture and sauté in melted butter until golden brown on each side.

MUSHROOM GARNISH

1½ pounds fresh mushrooms
Butter
1 large pimiento

1 tablespoon finely chopped parsley

Wash and slice mushrooms and sauté them in butter. Add pimiento, parsley, and season to taste.

SHALLOT SAUCE

2 tablespoons shallots, chopped fine
4 tablespoons butter
3 tablespoons flour
1 teaspoon salt

¼ teaspoon pepper
1 cup milk
1 cup chicken stock
Dash of cayenne (optional)
¼ cup sherry

Sauté shallots in butter until transparent. Gradually add flour, making a smooth paste. Add all but last ingredient, stirring continuously until sauce is thin and smooth. Add sherry and remove from heat.

Sautéed Asparagus and Snow Peas with Hazelnuts

2 quarts water
2 tablespoons salt
2 pounds asparagus
3 tablespoons vegetable oil
1½ cups hazelnuts
¼ teaspoon pepper
½ pound snow peas
½ cup chicken broth

Bring the water to a boil; add one tablespoon of salt. Cut the asparagus into 2-2½-inch pieces and blanch in hot boiling water for five minutes. Drain and run cold water over the asparagus so it won't continue cooking. Pour oil in frying pan and heat until hot. Then add hazelnuts, remaining salt, and pepper, and sauté for about one minute. Add asparagus and snow peas, stirring continuously to prevent burning. Pour in chicken broth and cook for five minutes or until tender. Adjust seasoning.

Skitch Henderson

Pianist and conductor

*M*usic director of the New York Pops, Skitch Henderson studied piano with Malcolm Frost and Roger Aubert, conducting with Albert Coates and Fritz Reiner, and harmony with Arnold Schoenberg. He makes frequent TV appearances and does guest conducting for various orchestras.

"I am English-born, Midwest-raised, and live happily in magnificent western Connecticut. We have a farm of some 250 acres with animals, flowers, dogs, cats, and smiling human beings. I am really a barbecue person at heart but because my wife, Ruth, is German, our cuisine is mixed."

BEEF RINDSROULADEN

"Serve with Knoedel or noodles and Bulgar rice."

6 slices ¼-inch-thick top round steak	12 teaspoons diced onion (white)
Mustard	12 teaspoons diced bacon
3 dill pickles sliced lengthwise in quarters	1 teaspoon flour
	1 pint sour cream
	¼ teaspoon marjoram

Pound meat with cleaver till thin. Spread with mustard. Use two pieces of pickle, two teaspoons of onion, and two teaspoons of bacon on one end of each piece of beef. Roll it, closing with toothpick or meat skewer. Brown meat rolls on all sides in butter or bacon fat. When dark brown, add one cup of water, cover pot, and let simmer for 40 minutes or until soft. Mix flour and sour cream, and add marjoram. Put meat rolls on preheated platter. Add sour cream mixture to liquid in pan, let it come to a boil, and remove immediately from heat. Serve with or over meat rolls.

German Pancakes (Eierkuchen)

"I prefer to make the Eierkuchen on the morning of the luncheon, but they can be made the day before and refrigerated, and will only be a little less light. The fricassee and berry sauce can both be made a day ahead."

5 cups flour	5 cups milk
½ teaspoon salt	½ pound butter, or more as
12 eggs	needed

Sift flour in a 5-quart bowl with salt. Make well in center. Beat eggs in a second 5-quart bowl. Add milk and blend. Transfer to a measuring cup. Pour egg mixture slowly into well while stirring continuously with a mixing spoon. Finish blending with whisk. (Do not use whisk in the beginning because batter is too thick.) Let stand at room temperature for approximately 1 hour. Stir again before using.

Heat a generous ounce (2 tablespoons) butter in a 10-inch omelet pan over high heat. Pour a scant ½ cup batter in pan and reduce heat to medium. Cook until golden brown on both sides, turning once. Add more butter to the pan as necessary and wipe out pan if butter begins to burn.

Slide onto a dinner plate. While next Eierkuchen is cooking, roll up the first one and place in a deep 18-inch oven-to-table baking dish. The pancakes must be rolled while still warm and flexible. Continue in this manner until all batter is used. There will be about 24 pancakes.

Cover dish with foil and reheat pancakes in a 250° oven before serving.

Serves 12.

Continued

Skitch Henderson *continued*

CHICKEN AND HAM FRICASSEE

FOR POACHING CHICKEN

2 whole carrots
1 shallot, peeled
1 stalk celery
4 sprigs fresh sage, or 1 teaspoon
  dry leaf

4 sprigs fresh marjoram, or
  1 teaspoon dry leaf
6 cups chicken stock or water
4 chicken breasts, skinned and
  boned

Bring all ingredients except chicken to a boil in a 5-quart pot and simmer 30 minutes. Add chicken breasts and simmer 5-10 minutes or until cooked. Remove breasts, cool, and dice. Strain broth and reserve.

FOR FRICASSEE

¾ cup butter
¾ cup flour
5 cups broth from poaching
Juice of ½ lemon
Diced, cooked chicken
3 cups baked ham, diced
1 cup prosciutto or Westphalian
  ham, diced

1 can (15 ounces) early June peas
  or 2 packages frozen
1 can (15 ounces) asparagus tips
  or 2 packages frozen
¼ cup parsley, finely chopped

Melt butter in a large sauté pan over medium heat. Add flour; cook and stir until roux is golden yellow. Add broth and whisk until smooth. Bring to a boil and simmer on a very low heat for 5 minutes. Add lemon juice, diced chicken, baked ham, and prosciutto and simmer 5 minutes more. Do not add salt; the saltiness of the ham should be plenty. Add vegetables and simmer again for 5 minutes (15 minutes total). Serve in a pottery casserole, or the pot you cook it in. Sprinkle with chopped parsley just before serving.

Fresh steamed vegetables or several varieties of mushrooms may be substituted for meats. This is the kind of dish everyone can put his or her personal stamp on.

Serves 12 as a sauce for German pancakes.

HOT FOUR-BERRY SAUCE

½ lemon with zest
1½ cups sugar, or to taste
1½ cups each blackberries,
   raspberries, currants or
   blueberries, and gooseberries,
   preferably fresh (If berries are
   canned or frozen in syrup, cook
   only with sugar to taste. Drain
   and rinse fruit canned in
   syrup.)

1½ ounces good brandy

Wash the lemon, cut into pieces, and put in a food processor with 1 cup of the sugar. Process with the steel knife until lemon is finely ground. Combine berries with the lemon mixture in a heavy pan. Add more sugar to taste. Cook over medium heat, stirring frequently, until juice appears. Then simmer for 30-60 minutes or until desired sauce texture is reached, still stirring frequently. Skim foam, if necessary, add brandy, and thereafter do not let boil. If necessary, reheat gently to below the simmer before serving.

Serves 12 as a sauce for German pancakes.

Edward Hoagland

Essayist, novelist, and travel writer

Edward Hoagland grew up in Fairfield County, Connecticut, and went to school in Deerfield, Massachusetts, and to college at Harvard. Since 1969 he has been spending from one-third to one-half the year in Barton, Vermont. Many of the 80 or so essays he has written in the past dozen years bear upon New England in one way or another, and particularly upon northeastern Vermont. He has published ten books, including *Walking the Dead Diamond River, The Courage of Turtles, Red Wolves and Black Bears, African Calliope,* and *Notes from the Century Before.*

"Here are a couple of recipes. I hope they suit. They are appropriately simple for a simplistic cook. The Spinach Pie was one my next-door neighbor on Wheeler Mountain in Barton, Vermont, taught me: Mrs. Wheeler, now dead ten years, but loved. The Salmon Chowder I picked up in Alaska in a Tlingit village on Admiralty Island called Angoon, while on the trail of John Muir. (But New England *did* have salmon, and will again.)"

SPINACH PIE

9-inch pie crust
2 pounds of fresh washed
  spinach, shredded and wilted
1 container (8 ounces) ricotta
  cheese
1 container (8 ounces) cottage
  cheese

2 eggs beaten with ¼ cup milk
1 teaspoon curry powder
1 teaspoon dry mustard
1 teaspoon cayenne
1 tablespoon soy sauce
Pinch of salt
Pepper to taste

Preheat oven to 425°. Line a 9-inch pie pan with pastry. Layer spinach, ricotta, and cottage cheese. Combine egg mixture with spices and pour over the top. Cover with an upper crust. Bake until crust is golden brown, about 45 minutes.

Serves 6-8.

SALMON CHOWDER

3 pounds salmon
Water (enough to cover fish)
1 bay leaf
1 sprig of parsley
3 peppercorns
¼ teaspoon salt

3 large potatoes, diced
¼ pound salt pork, diced
2 large onions, sliced
6 cups milk
Salt to taste
Pepper to taste

Place salmon in a deep pot; cover with water; add bay leaf, parsley, peppercorns, and salt; boil 15 minutes, or until salmon can be flaked with a fork and broth is cooked down. While salmon is cooking, boil potatoes and prepare pork and onions as follows: place pork in skillet; fry over medium flame 15 minutes, or until golden brown and well done; add onions and brown 5 minutes, stirring constantly. Remove cooked salmon and flake in large pieces. Heat deep soup tureen by letting it stand in very hot water. Place salmon, potatoes, onions, and salt pork in heated tureen; cover to keep hot. In a separate pot, heat milk to almost the boiling point; pour over hot ingredients; add salt and pepper. *Serves 6-8.*

Frederick E. Hood

Sailmaker

*B*orn and raised in Danvers, Massachusetts, Ted Hood moved to Marblehead in 1945, where he has lived ever since. In 1950 he founded Hood Sailmakers, Inc., now a worldwide business, and he is currently president of Hood Enterprises, Inc., which owns an active brokerage and yacht design operation and boatyard for storage, repair, and outfitting of new sailing yachts. Mr. Hood maintains an active interest in the sailmaking business and in Hood Yacht Systems, designers and builders of custom spars and marine hardware. He is a direct descendant of Richard Hood, one of the original settlers of Lynn and Nahant, Massachusetts, who emigrated from England in the 17th century.

BAKED STUFFED HADDOCK

"This is a recipe of my grandmother's and could well have been made in early New England days, with the following substitutions, which the early settlers would have had available: real chopped pickle, rather than pickle relish, and salt pork instead of bacon."

Allow ⅓ to ½ pound haddock (filleted and skinned) per person. Fillets shouldn't be too thick. Grease bottom of shallow baking dish. Place half of fish in bottom, cover with stuffing, cover with remaining half of fish, lay 2 or 3 strips of bacon on top. Bake about ½ hour at 350°. Serve with creamed egg sauce.

STUFFING
Melt butter, add ground common crackers, some sweet pickle relish, a little lemon juice, and a few drops of Tabasco.

Finnan Haddie

"This recipe my wife has experimented with over the years, and we often serve it when we entertain at brunch, or as a main course for dinner."

Thaw fish, cut into large chunks, place in vegetable steamer over unsalted water, and steam for 20-30 minutes. Drain in colander and pick carefully for bones. Make medium cream sauce; season with pepper and lots of paprika but no salt. Add fish and cut-up hard-boiled eggs.

Cherry Winks

"Dates are a favorite of mine. This is a recipe handed down from my wife's mother, and my wife has made them every Christmas since we've been married (27 years). I don't like really sweet desserts, and these aren't."

2¼ cups flour
1 teaspoon baking powder
½ teaspoon soda
½ teaspoon salt
¾ cup shortening
1 cup sugar
2 eggs
2 tablespoons milk

1 teaspoon vanilla
1 cup chopped pecans
1 cup chopped dates
⅓ cup chopped cherries
   (maraschino, not candied)
Extra cherries for decorating
2½ cups cornflakes, crushed

Sift together dry ingredients; combine shortening, sugar, eggs, milk, and vanilla. Blend in dry ingredients; mix well. Add pecans, dates, and cherries. Mix well. (*Hint:* Have dough well chilled, as it will be much easier to work with.) Shape into balls using a level tablespoon of dough for each cookie. Roll each ball of dough in cornflake crumbs. Place on greased cookie sheet. Top each cookie with ½ cherry. Bake at 375° for 10-12 minutes.

Makes 5 dozen.

Frances Minturn Howard

Writer and poet

"*B*y an unfortunate accident of travel, I was born in New Jersey, but all my ancestors on both sides hail from Rhode Island or Massachusetts. [They include Roger Williams and Julia Ward Howe, who was her great-grandmother.] I spent summers on Cape Cod as a child and now summer in a cottage we own in Rhode Island. I live in an old brick house on Beacon Hill, Boston, not too far from the gold dome of the State House.

"I write, compulsively. [She has had two books of poetry and two of prose published plus many articles and short stories in a variety of periodicals.] In my spare time I like to make jewelry; metalwork lets me use my hands, which I find much easier than using my head.

"I like swimming, gardening, walking, almost any kind of game. I am a little soft in the head about animals, and possess the most spoiled dog in Boston. I have a passion for the theatre, and have never seen a play so bad I would not sit through it. My birth sign is Pisces, which an aunt defined for me as 'Two fishes going in opposite directions and getting nowhere.'"

*   *   *   *   *

"My squash pie came about by a sort of evolution. We were living in Bedford, New Hampshire, during the Second World War, and had a victory garden in which we planted acorn squashes. The victory was all to the squashes; they won, hands down. Once planted, those squashes could not be stopped. Every time I looked out, another squash had burst from cover.

"I did my best with those squashes. I baked them, I boiled them, I fried them. I tried every recipe in the cookbooks. I attempted to give them away to the neighbors. But New Hampshire people know a thing or two and can defend themselves manfully against a brace of acorn squashes coming at them.

"At last, in desperation, I thought of making them into pies. To understand the full daring of this idea, you would have to know that I had never made any kind of pie in my life. Besides which, instead of sensibly using a boxed mix, I attempted for my first try something entitled Flaky Pastry. It turned out beautifully. What went into it required more thought.

"Most squash pies are, I think, rather watery affairs, a soft innocuous mass surrounded by a rim of hard cardboard. The very consistency of acorn squashes made mine a different matter. Acorn squashes are firm, compact, a mellow golden-brown in color and of a consistency, though delicate, you can really feel under your fork.

"I perused my cookbooks with carefree abandon and took what I liked from each. They said milk; I used light cream. Because I had so much squash, I doubled and tripled the squash mixture. But I also tripled the spices — all but the salt. All my cookbooks are sissy about spices, particularly ginger. A mass of bland substance like squash can absorb any quantity of ginger, and who wants a tasteless pie?

"Other changes occurred as I went along. 'You don't expect to make a respectable squash pie without brandy, do you?' my great-aunt said. The brandy couldn't be tasted as brandy but it added a wonderful rich taste to the mixture.

"My New Hampshire neighbors, like all good Yankees, adored squash pies. But they were taken by surprise by my acorn squash creations. They had thought you had to wait for the big winter squash to ripen.

"Anyone in their right mind would have. Cutting into an acorn squash is much the same as bisecting an armadillo; and after that you have to boil, scrape, mash, and strain it.

"I had picked the wrong type of pastry, too. A good solid biscuit crust would have been more appropriate and much easier to transport. My flaky pastry crumbled at a touch. But when your fork encountered it above the rich, firm, dark-brown filling, on which confectioner's sugar had been lightly sprinkled — well, my acorn squashes in the form of pies were never refused.

"Just before we left New Hampshire, a test of the culinary skills of all local piemakers occurred: the Fall cornhusking. For this event all the neighbors gathered and, after an afternoon of pleasant gossip and cornhusking, adjourned to the barn where long tables had been set up for a supper of good thick soup and pies contributed by local housewives.

"I had been eagerly looking forward to this event; the first time my pies had been publicly tested against local competitors. I had spent infinite time and effort on that pie, and that evening, seated at a long table next to my host, I waited anxiously as pie after pie appeared. Mine did not. A neighbor leaned across the table to ask, 'Where's your pie, Frances? I've been holding out for your pie. Didn't you make one?'

"I was opening my mouth to reply when I received a sharp kick in the ankle from my host.

" 'Shush!' he hissed. 'Not a word out of you. We weren't going to waste your pie on this mob. We ate it ourselves, for lunch.' "

Continued

Frances Minturn Howard *continued*

FRANCES HOWARD'S SQUASH PIE

"Now, in the city, I use packages of Birds Eye cooked squash instead of acorn. If raw squash, not frozen, is being used, the squash must first be cut up, boiled until soft, and then strained."

FLAKY PASTRY

2 cups sifted cake flour
¾ teaspoon salt
¾ cup shortening

1 tablespoon lemon juice beaten with egg yolk

Sift flour and salt together. Cut in shortening with two knives in crisscross motion, or with a pastry blender. Sprinkle lemon juice mixture, a little at a time, over mixture, working it in with fork till all particles are moistened and in small lumps. Roll out pastry, using light quick strokes. To prevent the crimped edge of pie from burning, set the pie plate on a piece of aluminum foil large enough to cover the edges.

SQUASH PIE

2 eggs, well beaten
¾ cup dark brown sugar, firmly packed
2 to 4 cups strained squash (if 4, double spices)
3 teaspoons ginger

4 teaspoons cinnamon
½ teaspoon salt
1 cup light cream (1½ if squash is doubled)
1 wine glass or jigger of good brandy

Combine ingredients, turn mixture into pie shell, and bake at 400° for 10 minutes, then 350° for 20 more. (Time depends on oven; advise testing pie with straw to determine firmness. Should be decently firm like a good custard, and will set a little more when taken out.)

Beatrice Trum Hunter

Author and lecturer

Natural foods cook and advocate Beatrice Trum Hunter is author of numerous articles and a dozen books about food and consumer issues, including *The Natural Foods Cookbook, Consumer Beware,* and *Gardening Without Poisons.* In addition, she has taught adult education classes; lectured at Boston University, the University of New Hampshire, and the University of Massachusetts; and given frequent demonstrations in natural foods preparation on the radio, at workshops and lectures, and on TV. A native New Yorker, Mrs. Hunter and her husband, John, summered in the Hillsboro, New Hampshire, area from 1948 until 1955, when they moved there permanently.

DATE ICE CREAM

"Ice creams are popular with most people in any season. This recipe uses no added sweetener of any kind. The dates provide all the sweetness desired. This is a healthful, easy-to-prepare, and delicious dessert. Since dates are available throughout the year, this recipe can be made and enjoyed at any time."

1½ cups dates, pitted
1 cup of water
1 cup of heavy cream, whipped

⅛ teaspoon ground mace (or cinnamon or cloves)

Quarter the dates and put into a blender. Add water and blend until puréed. Fold dates into the whipped cream, add the spice, and pour into 6 custard cups. Freeze.

Serves 6.

Continued

Beatrice Trum Hunter *continued*

FRUIT TORTEN

(Muerbe Teig, from Germany)

"This torten has many variations, depending on what fruits or berries are in season, or during the wintertime, what dried fruits are used. After the basic dough is placed in the pan, one section can be filled with one fruit or mixture of fruit, and another section with another fruit or mixture. In this way, it is easy to make two different desserts from the same recipe."

BASIC DOUGH

1 tablespoon of honey
¼ cup of oil
1 raw egg yolk

1 cup of whole wheat flour
Rind of 1 lemon, grated
Milk (if necessary)

Blend the honey, oil, and egg yolk. Stir in the flour and rind. Add a small amount of milk, if necessary, to make a stiff dough. Pat the dough to a depth of ¼ inch in an unoiled pan. Chill. Then spread with fruit filling.

FRUIT FILLING

1 pound dried apricots, prunes,
nectarines, apples, or peaches
(or a combination)

Soak the dried fruit overnight, drain, pit if necessary, and cut into pieces, reserving the juice for compote or fruit drinks. Or, use a proportionate amount of fresh berries or other fruit and cut if necessary, reserving the juice. After the fruit has been spread over the chilled basic dough, top with the custard.

CUSTARD

2 eggs
3 tablespoons of honey
1 teaspoon of pure vanilla extract

2 tablespoons whole milk or light
cream

In a blender, mix eggs, honey, vanilla extract, and milk or cream. Bake the torten for 20 minutes in a preheated oven at 375° and then at 300° for an additional 20-30 minutes until the custard on top is set. Serve hot or cold, adding a dab of yogurt or sour cream to each portion, if desired.

Serves 8.

Jill Ireland

TV and film actress

Born in London, England, Jill Ireland has lived in Windsor, Vermont, for the past 12 years with her husband, actor Charles Bronson, and their four children. When her acting profession doesn't demand out-of-state or -country commitments, Miss Ireland is busy running Zuleika Farm, where horses are bred for sale and trained for the hunter/jumper show ring, as well as for three-day events.

CHICKEN CURRY

"Serve with rice, coconut, raisins, peanuts, mango chutney, fried bananas, and yogurt."

4 onions, chopped
4 apples, skinned and diced
Oil
8 ounces margarine or butter
4 tablespoons curry powder
4 ounces flour
4 pints chicken stock
4 tomatoes, skinned and diced
2 bay leaves
2 cinnamon sticks
6 cloves
6 fluid ounces chutney
1 can (16 ounces) of pineapple pulp, drained
1 cup of green grapes, cut into halves
2 medium chickens, cut into pieces
¼ cup of oil

Sauté onions and apples in oil until brown. In separate saucepan, melt butter, add curry powder, and cook for 2 minutes; add flour and cook; add chicken stock a little at a time and bring to a boil between each addition. Add sauce to onion and apple mixture and simmer. Add remainder of ingredients, except the chicken and oil, and simmer slowly. Dust jointed chicken with a little flour and fry until lightly browned in the oil. Place chicken in casserole or baking dish, cover with the sauce, and cook in 350° oven for 1½-2 hours or until chicken is tender. Does not need salt or pepper.

David O. Ives

Vice Chairman, WGBH Educational Foundation

"*A* friend once nominated me as a successor to Parker Fennelly, who for years played the Yankee storekeeper in the Pepperidge Farm TV commercials. 'Perfect for the part,' he claimed. Whether I would have been or not, my credentials as a New Englander are certainly strong. I was born and brought up in Salem, Massachusetts, where both my father's and mother's family had lived for eight generations. I graduated from Milton Academy, Harvard College, and Harvard Business School. My life has been lived within a few miles of Boston except during World War II and from 1947-1955 when I was a journalist elsewhere in the country.

"Whether or not it is true, as some say, that 'the best thing about Boston is New England,' I have tried hard to take advantage of the fact that so much glorious country is nearby. I began sailing at Marblehead in a once-famous class of small catboats known as Brutal Beasts, and I have sailed the matchless Maine coast as well as the warm waters south of the Cape. In my salad days, I have climbed on skis to the top of Cannon Mountain in less time than it took to wait for the tramway to make the trip, but today it is only cross-country for me. And now I live in Cambridge only a 25-minute walk from my office at WGBH.

"In short, I am a New Englander and glad of it."

SAUSAGE RING

"This is a southern recipe my wife Patsy has used often, as it adapts so well to New England, using fall apples and sausage meat. It's delicious on a cold day. Perhaps it seems odd to suggest a southern recipe for a New England book, but believe me, we Yankees take to it."

2 pounds bulk sausage meat,
   extra hot
1½ cups cracker crumbs, rolled
   well
1 cup finely chopped apple

½ cup minced onion
2 eggs, beaten
½ cup milk
Salt to taste

Combine all ingredients in a bowl with a fork. Press the mixture into a buttered 6-cup ring mold. Turn the sausage ring out of the mold onto a shallow baking pan. Bake at 350° for one hour. Drain excess fat from the pan. Turn onto a round platter and arrange with hot biscuits or crackers around the ring. Place a knife on the platter so that guests may cut their own slices. Be sure to serve hot.

The sausage ring may be made ahead of time — cooked for ½ hour, then covered well and kept in the refrigerator for a day or two before the party. May also be frozen. Cook for remaining ½ hour before serving.

Lotte Jacobi

Photographer

*T*hrough her work as a portrait photographer and her photographs of theatre and dance during the 1920s and '30s in Berlin, Lotte Jacobi has come face to face with some of the most celebrated people in the world — Albert Einstein, Marc Chagall, Pablo Casals, Thomas Mann, Lotte Lenya, Peter Lorre, Robert Frost, Benjamin Britten, Eleanor Roosevelt, and the list goes on. A fourth-generation photographer (her great-grandfather learned from Daguerre), Miss Jacobi left Germany in 1935 to open a photography studio in New York City. Twenty years later she settled in Deering, New Hampshire, where she has been ever since. Miss Jacobi's photographs hang in public and private collections and continue to be exhibited in museums and galleries in this country and abroad.

"When I was young, I loved to cook and bake. Now, at 87, I selected a few things that I still like to do and that are the least complicated. Most other vegetables I like to eat raw. They taste so good that way; or I might steam some, like beans or brussels sprouts (one of my favorites)."

CABBAGE SOUP

1 small head white cabbage	¼ teaspoon thyme
3 tablespoons fat	¼ teaspoon marjoram
1 onion, chopped	¼ teaspoon pepper (or ¼ the
2 quarts rich meat stock	amount of cayenne pepper)
1 carrot, diced	2 tablespoons golden syrup

Cut the cabbage in small strips. Brown in fat with onion. Add the meat stock and simmer gently for about 2 hours. Strain a little of this stock into a small saucepan with the carrot, herbs, and pepper and cook for 15 minutes. Combine the two mixtures and add syrup. Bring to a boiling point and serve very hot. (You can add other herbs, wine vinegar.)   *Serves 6-8.*

HERBS HAMBURGER

2 pounds ground top round steak
¼ cup light cream
2 tablespoons grated onions
½ tablespoon Worcestershire
  sauce
½ teaspoon thyme
½ tablespoon garlic wine vinegar
1 teaspoon salt
½ teaspoon pepper

Blend all ingredients lightly but thoroughly with a fork. Form into loosely made cakes, about ½-inch thick. Sauté quickly in small amount of fat in a very hot pan, turning to brown both sides.   *Serves 5-6.*

RED CABBAGE

1 red cabbage
4 tart apples (sliced)
1 tablespoon basil wine vinegar
⅓ cup (or a little less) honey or
  sugar
1 cup red wine

Shred cabbage very fine; put in heavy kettle with all the other ingredients, except the wine. Cover tightly and simmer for about 1½ hours. Add wine and let it cook slowly for ¾ hour longer.

Justin Kaplan
Author and lecturer

Recipient of the Pulitzer Prize for biography and the National Book Award, Justin Kaplan has contributed to numerous publications, among them *The Atlantic Monthly, Boston Globe, American Scholar, New York Times, Washington Post,* and *New Republic.* His books include *Lincoln Steffens: A Biography, Mr. Clemens and Mark Twain,* and *Walt Whitman: A Life.* He most recently was editor of *Walt Whitman: Complete Poetry and Collected Prose.* Mr. Kaplan lives in Cambridge with his wife, novelist Anne Bernays, and their children.

"I spent six or seven years here in Cambridge as an undergraduate and graduate student [at Harvard], went back to New York to follow a writing and publishing career, and when I decided to become a full-time writer, the choice of New England seemed inevitable. Partly it's Widener Library at Harvard that drew me back, but there are many other things."

GREAT SOUP

"This is a simple dish we first prepared years ago and have been enjoying ever since, especially during the summer. It's good at breakfast, too."

Combine one can of jellied consommé and an equivalent amount of plain yogurt. Season with lemon juice, black pepper, and dill weed (or fresh dill). A little garnish of red or black caviar won't hurt.

Rose Fitzgerald Kennedy

Humanitarian

If asked what kind of career she would have liked, Rose Kennedy would probably say the very one she has had — as wife and mother. Born in Boston in 1890, she and Joseph P. Kennedy, to whom she was married for 55 years, had nine children, three of whom became prominent political figures. To members of her family she must certainly provide an admirable role model, to those outside the family, an inspiration of how to look at life and all that unfolds — appreciate the good and accept the unexplainable.

OLD-FASHIONED SUGAR COOKIES

½ cup butter (sweet, unsalted)
¾ cup sugar
3 egg yolks
½ teaspoon vanilla

1 tablespoon cream or milk
1¼ cups flour (Pillsbury)
¼ teaspoon salt
¼ teaspoon baking powder

Cream butter until light and fluffy. Beat in sugar. Add egg yolks and vanilla and beat thoroughly. Add cream. Sift dry ingredients together and stir into mixture. Mix well and arrange by teaspoonfuls on a buttered cookie sheet, 1 inch apart. Bake about 8 minutes at 375°. *Makes 50 to 60 cookies.*

Continued

Rose Kennedy *continued*

BOSTON CREAM PIE

CREAM SPONGE CAKE

1 cup pastry flour
4 egg whites
1 cup granulated sugar
4 egg yolks
1½ tablespoons cold water

1½ tablespoons lemon juice
1 teaspoon vanilla
1⅓ teaspoons baking powder
Salt

Sift flour 3 times. Beat egg whites until stiff, but not dry, and fold in one half the quantity of sugar gradually.

Beat egg yolks and liquids, and continue to beat until very thick and pale yellow. Beat in remaining sugar.

Combine yolks and whites, folding together until the mixture is blended. Sift in flour, baking powder, and salt, cutting and folding into the egg mixture. Pour into buttered pan. Bake in moderately slow oven (325°) for one hour.

ICING

3 tablespoons cornstarch
⅔ cup granulated sugar
Salt
3 egg yolks

1½ cups milk, scalded
2 tablespoons butter
1 teaspoon vanilla
Confectioners sugar

Split the cream sponge cake into 2 layers after it has been kept 24 hours. Mix cornstarch, sugar, and salt. Beat egg yolks until thick and combine with cornstarch mixture, beating until perfectly smooth. Pour on hot milk, gradually adding butter and vanilla. Cook in the top of a double boiler until thick, stirring all the time to prevent lumping. Spread between the cake layers and sift on confectioners sugar.   *Serves 6.*

Stephen King

Novelist

Novelist Stephen King washed clothes profession-ally, pumped gas, and worked in textile mills before he began writing horror stories for a living. Born in Portland, Maine, he has spent most of his life in that state. He currently lives in Bangor during the winter and Center Lovell during the summer, along with his wife, Tabitha (author of *Small World* and *Caretakers*), and their three children. A prolific writer (and member of The American Vampire Society), Mr. King once had three novels on the best-sellers lists at the same time. Many of his books, which include *Carrie, Salem's Lot, The Shining, Firestarter, Cujo,* and *Christine,* have been filmed or are currently scheduled for motion picture production.

BASIC BREAD

"Baking bread is one of the ways I relax. I like kneading it, and I love the smell of it, the way it fills the house and makes your mouth water."

2 packages of dry yeast dissolved in ¾ cup of warm (not hot) water, with sugar as directed on the package
2 cups lukewarm milk
3 tablespoons sugar
1 tablespoon salt
3 tablespoons shortening
8 cups of flour, all-purpose or bread flour
Melted butter

Dissolve yeast. Add milk, sugar, salt, shortening, and half the flour; mix until smooth. Mix in rest of flour until dough is easy to handle. Knead on floured surface until smooth — 10 minutes should do it. Put in greased bowl, cover with dish towel, and let it rise about an hour, until double. Divide dough in half, shape into loaves, place in greased loaf pans, brush with butter, and let rise another hour. Cook at 425° about 25-30 minutes, until brown. To test for doneness, tap to see if they sound hollow. Brush with butter if you like.

Continued

Stephen King *continued*

LUNCHTIME GLOOP

"My kids love this. I only make it when my wife, Tabby, isn't home. She won't eat it, in fact doesn't even like to look at it."

2 cans Franco American
Spaghetti (without meatballs)

1 pound cheap, greasy hamburger

Brown hamburg in large skillet. Add Franco American Spaghetti and cook till heated through. Do not drain hamburg, or it won't be properly greasy. Burn on pan if you want — that will only improve the flavor. Serve with buttered Wonder Bread.

EGG PUFF

"This is Tabby's recipe, and she often makes it for breakfast. She says a little chopped ham spices it up nicely."

2 tablespoons butter
4 eggs
$\frac{2}{3}$ cup flour
$\frac{2}{3}$ cup whole milk

1 tablespoon sugar
1 teaspoon salt
$\frac{1}{2}$ cup diced ham (optional)

Melt butter in oven-proof skillet in 400° oven. Beat eggs, flour, milk, sugar, and salt until smooth. Add ham if you like. Take skillet from oven with oven mitt. Put mix in skillet and return to oven for 15-20 minutes.

Serves 4, and can be divided in two easily.

Maxine Kumin

Poet and novelist

axine Kumin's poems have appeared in publications throughout
the country. In 1973 she received the Pulitzer Prize for poetry for
her book *Up Country.*
"Though born in Philadelphia, I came to New England at an early age
(seventeen) to attend Radcliffe College, married a Harvard man, and never
went back to the Middle Atlantic states. We lived for many years in a
suburb of Boston, but bought this old farm [in New Hampshire] in 1963,
after it had stood empty for six years. For twenty years we have been
restoring it and reclaiming the pastures, which had reverted to woodlands.
In 1976, we moved here as permanent year-rounders. We live at the dead-
end top of a hill, on a dirt road off a dirt road, two miles from town, in
Warner, with, at the moment, five horses, and two more in the planning
stages.

"Since we put out about fifty taps each spring and neighbors sugar off
for us, we always have an abundance of maple syrup — enough to cook
with as well as enjoy over waffles and corn fritters. That accounts for the
maple syrup in both recipes. And, usually by the end of February, I am
faced with a cluster of winter squashes that are beginning to show signs of
doom. Hence the squash bread. (There is no excuse for the blueberries,
except to say that we love them.)"

SQUASH BREAD

½ cup vegetable oil
2 large eggs
1 cup maple syrup
1⅔ cups flour
½ teaspoon baking powder
1 teaspoon baking soda
½ teaspoon salt

½ teaspoon cinnamon
1 teaspoon nutmeg
½ teaspoon ginger
1 cup mashed squash, well
 drained
½ cup chopped nuts
1 cup raisins

Beat oil, eggs, and maple syrup until eggs are foamy. Add flour, baking
powder, soda, salt, and spices. Stir in squash, nuts, and raisins, and bake in
a greased bread pan at 350° for 75 minutes or more, testing for doneness
and dryness. This is probably well enough cooked at 65 minutes, if you like
a moist loaf. (I usually double this recipe and do two loaves at a time.)

Continued

Maxine Kumin *continued*

BLUEBERRY BUCKLE

½ stick butter or margarine
⅔ cup maple syrup
¼ cup lemon juice
1 large egg
1⅔ cups flour
½ teaspoon salt

2 teaspoons baking powder
3 cups blueberries (previously
    mixed with ⅓ cup flour to keep
    them from sinking to the
    bottom of the baking dish)

Melt butter in large ovenproof bowl. Beat into it maple syrup, lemon juice, and egg. Sift into this the flour, salt, and baking powder; stir in blueberries. Spread this stiff batter into a baking dish approximately 12″ x 7″ (I use a glass one), well greased. Sprinkle with crumb topping, and bake at 350° for 45-55 minutes. Test for doneness with a toothpick. Best served warm, but this also freezes well.

CRUMB TOPPING

½ cup brown sugar
⅓ cup flour

1 teaspoon cinnamon
½ stick butter or margarine

Mix in small bowl with pastry cutter.

Irving R. Levine

News reporter and commentator

*I*rving R. Levine has been an NBC News correspondent for more than 30 years. A native of Pawtucket, Rhode Island, and graduate of Brown and Columbia Universities, Mr. Levine began his journalism career with the *Providence* (Rhode Island) *Journal-Bulletin*. He has written four books, contributed articles to a number of national magazines, and is a frequent lecturer. He currently lives in Washington, D.C., with his wife and three children.

"These recipes have been handed down but not through the generations. I received them from a friend, who received them from a friend. The reasons I have chosen them are that they are quick, easy-to-make, and delicious!"

COCKTAIL MEATBALLS

These can be frozen and kept on hand for spur-of-the-moment occasions.

1 tablespoon minced onion	3 tablespoons brown sugar
1 can cranberry sauce	2 pounds ground meat, shaped
1 can tomato soup	into small meatballs

Sauté onion in a heavy saucepan. Add other ingredients, except the meatballs, and mix well. Then add meatballs, cover, and allow to cook in sauce over low heat for half an hour.

Continued

Irving R. Levine *continued*

QUICK FROZEN CHOCOLATE MOUSSE

"This is a delightful, easy-to-make dessert. For a heavenly variation, thaw mousse and alternate scoops of softened mousse with scoops of softened vanilla ice cream in dessert glasses. It is wonderful!"

2 bars (3¾ ounces each) milk
chocolate
¼ cup water

¼ teaspoon orange (or lemon)
extract
1 pint heavy cream

In a double boiler, melt bars of milk chocolate with water. Stir constantly until chocolate melts. Cool—but not until thick — and add extract.

In a large bowl, whip heavy cream until stiff. Fold into chocolate, then freeze in pot de crème cups or a soufflé dish. Remove from freezer 45 minutes to 1 hour before serving.

Robert J. Lurtsema

Radio host and producer

Since October of 1971, Robert J. Lurtsema has been host and producer of WGBH Radio's "Morning Pro Musica" program, which is broadcast every day from 7 A.M. until noon. Born in Cambridge, Massachusetts, and currently residing in Wellesley, Mr. Lurtsema has lived in the Boston area most of his life. He graduated from Boston University, where he studied drama, radio and television, and journalism, and has worked as an actor, director, lumberjack, carpenter, journalist, and advertising executive. In addition to his seven-days-a-week commitment to his radio program, Mr. Lurtsema sits on the boards of directors of more than 20 musical organizations, contributes time to benefits for groups concerned with peace and the environment, and pursues his many interests—acting, writing, painting, and photography among them.

"The hardest part of coming up with a recipe is taking the time to measure and write down what I do. The second hardest part is dreaming up a name for it. I cook purely by instinct, a process that usually begins with browsing through a supermarket until something catches my fancy, then seeking out what seems as though it would combine well with that. At home I skim through the leftovers for anything that needs to be used up and can be thrown in without doing too much damage, scan the herbs and spices for whatever seems as though it will best accent the basic flavor, and then proceed simply by yielding to the impulse of the moment. Most of the time it works. The major disadvantage is that when it works superbly, there's little likelihood that I'll ever be able to do it exactly the same way again. *C'est la vie.* Gustatory ecstasy is an ephemeral experience."

Chicken Siam

10 ounces peeled pearl onions	½ teaspoon ginger
¼ cup slivered almonds	1 teaspoon ground sage
¼ cup soy sauce	4 cups (10 medium stalks)
2 pounds chicken thighs	chinese cabbage
8 ounces water chestnuts	1 teaspoon ground mint leaves
½ teaspoon galanga powder	3 cups bean sprouts
(Thai)	Salt and pepper

Continued

Robert J. Lurtsema *continued*

Snip ends from pearl onions, peel, and parboil. Blanch slivered almonds. Heat soy sauce in large skillet and stir in onions and almonds with 1 cup of water (from parboiled onions). Add chicken, water chestnuts, galanga powder, ginger, sage, and chinese cabbage and stir. Sprinkle top with mint leaves, cover, and steam 20 minutes. Add bean sprouts, cover, and steam another 10 minutes. Salt and pepper to taste just before serving.

Serves 6.

ORANGE-MAPLE ACORN SQUASH

1 large acorn squash
½ cup orange juice (or 3 fresh squeezed oranges)

1 small cinnamon stick
¼ cup maple syrup

Cut squash in half, remove seeds, and place, cut side down, in shallow pan containing about an inch of water. Bake for 1 hour (until it loses hardness) in 350° oven. Stir orange juice with cinnamon stick over heat almost to point of boiling, then stir in maple syrup. Remove pulp from shells and mash with fork. Add in maple-orange mixture and reheat, if necessary, on stove top or in oven.

Serves 2.

"Please note: These two recipes are terrific together."

M-R

*Clockwise from top: Bill Rodgers, Edmund Muskie,
Ed McMahon, Estelle Parsons*

Margaret Manning
Book editor

Robert Manning
Journalist and editor

Margaret Manning's paternal ancestors came to New England from England in 1630 and lived in and around Salem. During the 1880s, both her grandmother's and her grandfather's families moved West — her grandmother in a covered wagon, her grandfather on horseback. They did not meet each other until some years later in South Dakota. Mrs. Manning is book editor of *The Boston Globe* and has lived in Massachusetts since 1964.

Robert Manning is editor-in-chief of Boston Publishing Company, publisher of *The Vietnam Experience,* a 16-volume illustrated history of U.S. involvement in Vietnam. Born in upstate New York, he moved to Cambridge, Massachusetts, in 1964 and to Boston in 1971, where he and his wife, Margaret, still live. A former Nieman Fellow and Fellow at the Institute of Politics at Harvard University, Mr. Manning was Assistant Secretary of State from 1962 to 1964 and editor-in-chief of *The Atlantic Monthly* from 1964 to 1980.

MARGARET MANNING'S FISH SOUP

"You can use any kind of fish for this recipe as long as it is fresh."

Use fish stock made with fish scraps, sliced onions and carrots, dry white wine and water, salt, pepper, and parsley, etc. and then strained. Put whatever fish you have (flounder, haddock, bluefish, sea perch, bass, schrod), cut into two-inch pieces, into the strained, boiling stock and simmer for five minutes. Meanwhile, you have sautéed a substantial amount of sliced onions or leeks, or both, as well as peeled and chopped tomatoes and lots of pressed garlic. Put that, more or less cooked, in with the fish and stock. Add some lemon peel, grated or chopped finely, and a bouquet garni, plus some saffron, salt, pepper, and Tabasco if, like us, you favor some heat in the dish. Let all this simmer for about 10 minutes and then if you like add some scallops and/or shrimps. Top each dish or bowl of soup with parsley and serve with garlic bread.

Mexican Pizza

"This makes a pleasant lunch with jug wine or beer. One of these is pretty filling, but I sometimes like to split a second with somebody."

Fry corn tortillas (which can be kept frozen), one per person, in corn or vegetable oil until crisp; drain them on paper towels. Spread each with refried beans, brush with hot chili sauce (we use El Paso beans and hot sauce), and sprinkle with a mixture of diced cheddar and Monterey Jack cheese, then chopped green pepper and shreds of lettuce. For variety you can add thin slices of pepperoni. Place the pizzas in the oven, preheated to 350°, until the cheese melts and bubbles.

Jumbo Shrimp

"This is a great lunch or after theatre supper. It's not a dinner unless you are dining à deux."

Clean and arrange in a casserole 4 to 5 jumbo shrimp per person. Melt enough butter — according to number of shrimp and this dish needs a lot — and cook in it enough garlic, cut up. We love garlic but this is a matter of taste. Remove garlic. Add salt, pepper, Worcestershire sauce, and oregano. Pour sauce over shrimp and bake in 450° oven for 20 minutes (15 minutes if shrimp are small). Garnish with cut-up parsley on top. Serve with rice (the garlic butter sauce flavors the rice) and salad.

Baked Haddock

"This recipe is infinitely expandable, is delicious and so easy it is probably a criminal offense."

Put haddock filets in an ovenproof dish. (I usually have the skin taken off, but it's not necessary.) Slice onion very thinly and strew on top. (One onion is enough for 2 filets.) Make a sauce with lemon juice, Worcestershire sauce, and Dijon mustard — salt and pepper, if desired. Dump that in or on. Spread a blanket of sour cream over the lot and bake at 400° for 15 or 20 minutes, depending on thickness of filets.

Continued

Margaret & Robert Manning *continued*

STUFFED ROAST LEG OF LAMB

"This is an expensive meal and therefore suitable only for expensive occasions."

Have butcher trim and bone leg without butterflying it so that there is a cavity at each end. Marinate in 3 cups red wine, 1 cup brown stock (made of beef shanks, veal shanks, sliced onions, carrots, salt, parsley, and thyme), another sliced onion, rosemary, salt, pepper, and whatever. After 12 or more hours remove lamb, pat dry, and keep marinade.

In food processor grind half pound boneless veal and several cloves garlic according to taste; add a quarter cup of cream and an egg, and add this, well blended, to a third cup fresh bread crumbs and some Parmesan cheese and minced shallot or scallion, and salt and pepper. This is the stuffing.

Sprinkle cavity of the lamb with salt, pepper, and lemon juice. Sew up the small end of the cavity. Stuffing goes in the larger end which is then sewed up as well. Tie, or perhaps truss is a better word, the lamb at one-inch intervals with string. Rub it with olive oil and rosemary, then with salt and pepper. Roast (in roasting pan, of course) in middle of a preheated oven at 500° for 10 minutes; reduce heat to 325° and roast for 13-15 minutes per pound (boned) or until a meat thermometer says 130° for medium rare meat. Take lamb out of oven and leave on heated platter for 15-20 minutes.

While lamb is roasting, reduce marinade to about 2 cups. Strain. Pour fat from roasting pan (now you are in the last furlong) into a bowl and deglaze the roasting pan with the reduced marinade. Put into a saucepan (adding pressed garlic if you wish) and boil. You can thicken this sauce with a beurre manié if you like thickened sauce but it is not really necessary. Serve sauce with sliced lamb. *Serves 6-8.*

BAKED PEARS

Cut pears in half. Peel and scoop out seeds. Cut small slice off bottom of each so they will lie flat in baking dish. Sprinkle with lemon juice. On each pear put a tablespoon or so of melted butter and a tablespoon of sugar. Bake in 350° oven for 40 or 50 minutes, less if pears are ripe. Baste. When done put pears in serving dish. Cook butter and sugar remaining in baking dish over low flame until it caramelizes well. Then add some heavy cream. Heat the sauce and pour over pears.

Maxwell Mays

Artist

Maxwell Mays did his first *Yankee* magazine cover in 1964 and there have been many more since that time. Born in Providence, Rhode Island, Mr. Mays has lived in Europe, South America, California, and New York City. "I live in a 1727 farmhouse, an historic landmark in the western hills of Rhode Island. There is a big fireplace in the kitchen which burns cordwood, and sometimes cookery 'as went wrong.' "

* * * * *

"These food ideas are from a talk I gave quite a few times called 'Artists Like to Eat "Good." ' They come from any number of 'starving artists' who would come to the studio door with a good fat glass of jug wine and a big welcoming smile. A party for artists stays at the table until the town hall clock strikes midnight. It's the same with artists' gatherings in Cornwall, England; Milan, Italy; Provincetown, U.S.A. . . . Artists are very special people and they don't fool about food! Artists always cook with a big spoon, a warm smile, and love in their hearts. Artists' parties are special . . . and what I am saying is get to know some artists and get yourself invited to share a crusty loaf!"

HEARTY PORTUGUESE SOUP

"This has a great affinity for being eaten with the round yellow loaf of Portuguese sweet bread (warmed). It also is very good indeed with corn bread. Recommended: a lettuce salad with red onion slices and black olives. If you feel you can add water and lengthen this soup, ask more people in."

In a Dutch oven sear a pound of stew beef in a puddle of light olive oil. Cook until transparent 2 large sliced onions with the beef. Add 1 can consommé and 2 cans of water, 1 stalk celery, 2 or 3 (or 4) garlic cloves (squashed and pressed), 1 can stewed tomatoes, salt and pepper, and a can of kidney beans. Add a package of frozen chopped spinach and a pound of linguiça sausage cut into 1-inch chunks. This can be expanded by adding more of any single or all of the ingredients. The secret flavoring is in the linguiça.

Continued

Maxwell Mays *continued*

LAMB KIDNEYS IN BURGUNDY

"Serve very hot with strips of buttered toast."

12 lamb kidneys
2 ounces butter
1 tablespoon flour
3 tablespoons chopped parsley
1 clove garlic, through the press

Burgundy
Salt
Fresh black pepper from the grinder

Split, skin, and remove the white core from the kidneys. Heat butter and sauté the halved kidneys, quickly searing both sides to keep tender. Sprinkle 1 tablespoon flour over them and stir; add parsley and garlic, then add the wine which has been cut with water *and heated.* Salt and pepper to taste. Turn down flame, cover skillet, and cook for ½ hour stirring frequently.

BAKED KIDNEY BEANS PAYSANNE

"This dish can be made with canned kidney beans, to save the time usually required to cook the dried beans."

Chop one large onion and fry in butter. Add diced, smoked, or raw ham and mix with the onion. Sprinkle a little flour over all and add half a cup of canned consommé and one cup of the red wine you will be serving for dinner. Salt and cayenne. Cook for ten minutes, then add one large can of kidney beans and mix well in the sauce. Put in a baking dish, place strips of bacon over the top, and bake for half an hour.

CHICKEN SAUTÉ ARCHIDUC

"A dinner for two and quickly prepared. This one comes from a young artist friend, who tells me he 'cooks for seduction!' . . . This should take only twenty minutes but needs constant attention. Don't answer the telephone."

1 two-pound chicken cut up for sauté	2 chopped white onions
2 ounces butter	2 ounces white wine
Salt	Paprika
	½ cup sweet cream

Sauté chicken in 2 ounces of butter and shake to sear evenly. Add salt and onions that have been "melted" separately, but not browned. Add the white wine and, after wine has reduced a little and all of the ingredients are well blended, dust with plenty of paprika, Spanish or Hungarian. (Get some new, don't trust an old faded supply.) Mix well and pour cream over all; heat and serve with the thinnest slices of cucumber.

Gregory Mcdonald

Novelist

Harvard graduate (class of '58), recipient of the Poe Award (1975 and 1977), and former editor and critic with *The Boston Globe,* Gregory Mcdonald is author of two successful mystery series, one starring "Fletch" and the other "Flynn." The books have sold worldwide. Born in Shrewsbury, Massachusetts, and a descendant of the settlers of the Springfield Valley, Mr. Mcdonald has sailed extensively the coasts of North America (particularly New England), Latin America, and Europe. He lives in Massachusetts with his wife, Susan, and their two sons.

LOCRO

(An Andean potato soup)

"Last summer, walking in the Peruvian and Ecuadorean Andes with our friends, the Tomas Kohn family, Susi and I became quite taken by locro, *a potato soup as available there as fast food is here. A woman with child slung on her back keeps a pot of it warm on every street corner. If you stop for gasoline in the truck you can buy a bowl of* locro *for a few pennies. Needless to say, the ingredients vary as does the taste, but the enclosed recipe is about right. Potatoes there are more yellow than here, so appearance, and taste, cannot be exactly duplicated."*

4 cups water	½ cup milk
4 pounds potatoes	½ cup cream
8 scallions (whole)	5 ounces of mozzarella cheese, grated
1 teaspoon salt	
Pepper to taste	1 tablespoon of Parmesan cheese, grated
4 cabbage leaves	
1 stalk parsley	

Boil the water. Add the potatoes cut into thirds. Add scallions, salt and pepper, cabbage, and parsley. Cook down potatoes until soft. Remove scallions and parsley. Cook until potatoes fall apart into soup. Add milk, cream, and grated cheeses at last minute.

AJI

(A Latin American piquancy)

"I enjoy Aji at most meals in Latin America, yet am never served it in North America. It is a pleasant piquancy which can improve almost any meal, and not just the entrée. A dash can even be placed on the tops of most soups."

Red pepper
Water
Scallions

Parsley
Tree tomatoes (if available)

Parboil red pepper one minute. It is important that you discard this water entirely. Place red pepper in food processor with ½ cup water. Add scallions, parsley, and tree tomatoes, if available. Mince finely. Serve in small condiment dish with entrée.

GREGORY MCDONALD'S HAM AND CHEESE SANDWICH

"My breadless ham-and-cheese sandwich derives partly from my Scottish blood (What to do with the juice in the watermelon rind jar?), my sweet tooth, my feeling that wind-blown bread does little to enhance most sandwiches, and, frankly, my lazy desire to have prepared snacks in the refrigerator so that hunger, while working, may be sated without interruption of the most basic of all intellectual questions, What to eat?"

1 pound Philadelphia cream
  cheese
1 pound pressed ham slices

1 jar commercial watermelon
  rind
Toothpicks

Place cream cheese in bowl at room temperature. Stir only the leftover juice from a jar of watermelon rind into the cheese. Spread cheese/juice mix generously onto ham slice. Roll the slice into sausage shape and pin together with toothpicks. Chill and serve as lunch, late-night, or picnic snack.

Ed McMahon

TV announcer and actor

*E*d McMahon grew up in Lowell, Massachusetts, attended Boston College, and started his radio career in Lowell at station WLLH. He joined "The Tonight Show" in 1962, when Johnny Carson took over as host, and has been the program's announcer ever since. In addition, he has appeared on Broadway, in motion pictures, and in TV movies and other shows.

Loin of Pork

Wash and dry pork loin, then cover with seasoned salt. Alternate on top (using skewers) slices of onion and parsley. Roast in normal fashion.

During last 45 minutes of cooking, baste frequently with Grand Marnier. This adds a delightful flavor to the pork and makes an incredibly good gravy.

Serve with scalloped apples and corn pudding.

Ed's Favorite Dessert

Haagen-daz carob ice cream
Haagen-daz vanilla ice cream

Banana liqueur

Pour liqueur over the ice cream and serve with Pogen cookie stick and whipped cream. Enjoy.

Edmund S. Muskie

Statesman

Edmund Muskie was born in Rumford, Maine. Educated at Bates College and Cornell University Law School, he served in the Maine House of Representatives, as governor of Maine, and in the U.S. Senate. On May 8, 1980, he was sworn in as the 58th secretary of state and served until January 1981. Mr. Muskie and his wife, Jane, currently reside in Washington, D.C., where he is a senior partner with an international law firm. The Muskies have five children and three grandchildren and try to spend as much time as possible at their family home in Kennebunk Beach, Maine.

CRAB CAKES

"This recipe was given to our family by Kitty Baxter, a dear friend who lives in an 18th-century house in historic Chestertown on the eastern shore of Maryland."

1 egg	Dash of Worcestershire sauce
1 heaping tablespoon mayonnaise	1 pound crab meat, shells
1 heaping tablespoon Dijon	removed
mustard	Buttered cracker crumbs
Salt and pepper	

Beat first five ingredients together with fork. Add crab meat and form mixture into patties the size of medium hamburgers. Coat with buttered cracker crumbs and fry in Teflon pan for 5 minutes each side. Do not overcook!

Continued

Edmund Muskie *continued*

POLISH MEATLOAF

Although Jane Muskie claims she was not patient enough to learn to prepare most of her husband's mother's recipes, she finds this one to be not only simple, but also well liked by all the Muskie children.

1½ pounds ground chuck	1 egg
1 cup cracker crumbs *or* 2 cups bread crumbs	1 medium-size onion, chopped
	2 teaspoons milk

Mix all together until well blended and make into *large* patties. Brown on high heat in electric fry pan or large heavy fry pan and then lower heat. Cover and simmer, adding small amounts of water every now and then. You should gradually accumulate 2 or 3 cups of browned juice. Test after 45 minutes to see if meat has cooked to your taste. Cook longer if needed. Thicken juice and serve over patties.

Scott and Helen Nearing

Authors and organic farmers

"Scott and I lived (and farmed) for 19 years in Jamaica, Vermont. We earned our living making maple syrup and sugar and raised our own food in extensive gardens. When our quiet valley became rife with city ski-types, we removed to a more isolated spot in a tiny village on the shores of Penobscot Bay in Maine. Here we raised blueberries and again gardened. We've lived in Harborside since 1953 — probably still looked on as city folk ourselves."

(Scott Nearing died in August 1983, just before his 100th birthday. A former teacher of economics, he wrote six books with his wife, Helen, about the back-to-the-land movement and 50 books of his own, ranging from economics to his autobiography.)

HORSE CHOW

Helen Nearing's favorite recipe is a cookless one. "I've put together 299 other recipes in my Simple Food for the Good Life. *It's intended for the use of people of moderate fortune who do not affect magnificence in their style of living."*

4 cups old-fashioned rolled oats
½ cup raisins
Juice of half a lemon

Dash of sea salt
Sufficient olive oil or other
   vegetable oil to moisten

Mix all together and consume with wooden spoons out of wooden bowls.

Thomas P. O'Neill, Jr.

Speaker of the U.S. House of Representatives

*T*homas P. (Tip) O'Neill, Jr., has served as Speaker of the United States House of Representatives since January 4, 1977. Born and raised in Cambridge, Massachusetts, he graduated from Boston College in 1936 and began his political career the same year when he was elected to the Massachusetts House of Representatives. Mr. O'Neill and his wife, Millie, have five children and seven grandchildren. Their summer home is in Harwichport, on Cape Cod, where they spend most of their leisure time from May through October each year.

BEAN SOUP

(Served in the U.S. House of Representatives Restaurant)

2 pounds No. 1 white Michigan beans	Salt and pepper
Water	Smoked ham hock

Cover beans with cold water and soak overnight. Drain and re-cover with water. Add a smoked ham hock and *simmer slowly* for about four hours until beans are cooked tender. Then add salt and pepper to suit taste. Just before serving, bruise beans with large spoon or ladle, enough to cloud.

Serves 6.

Cape Cod Fish Chowder

"Fish has always been a favorite of mine . . . fresh from the markets in Boston. Fish chowder is a particular favorite and I've enjoyed it for as long as I can remember. Jimmy's Harborside has the best fish chowder in the world, I think, and whenever I have an opportunity to dine there I always have it. We have enjoyed this recipe for many years — it is easy to make and we like lots of fresh fish in it and not much of anything else!"

3 pounds fresh cod fillets
¼ pound salt pork
3 large yellow onions, sliced thin
4 cups raw potatoes, sliced thin
4 cups boiling water
4 cups milk
Salt and pepper

Slice fillets in 2-inch pieces. Dice salt pork; fry slowly in heavy skillet until crisp. Remove pork and save. Cook onions in pork fat until soft. Add potatoes to boiling water — cook until tender. Add fish — cook about 15 minutes. Add onions and milk and season with salt and pepper to taste. Heat to serving temperature, but do not boil. Garnish with cooked diced salt pork. Serve with pilot crackers. *Serves 8.*

Bobby Orr

Hockey player

Bobby Orr was a defenseman for the Boston Bruins from 1966 to 1975. During that time he led his team to two Stanley Cup victories. He then played for the Chicago Black Hawks until his retirement from hockey in 1979. Bobby has been associated with Nabisco Brands, Inc. for many years and is now the vice president of sales and marketing/U.S.A. and Canada for Pandick Press, Inc., the financial printer. In addition, he is on the board of directors of Cullinet, Inc., a computer software company, and contributes much of his time to numerous fund-raising events. Bobby currently lives in a suburb of Boston with his wife, Peggy, and two sons, Darren and Brent.

BOBBY'S CHILI

1 large onion, coarsely chopped
1 large green pepper, coarsely chopped
2 garlic cloves, mashed
1 pound lean hamburger

2 packages chili season mix
1 large can of baked kidney beans
1 can regular kidney beans
1 large can tomato sauce
1 teaspoon chili powder

Sauté onion, green pepper, and garlic in a small amount of butter. Set aside. Brown hamburger meat in the drippings from above and drain off excess fat. Put all the ingredients prepared thus far in a large pot. Stir in chili season mix, kidney beans, tomato sauce, and chili powder. Simmer in covered pot for 1½ hours. If chili is too thick, add a little water.

SWEDISH MEATBALLS

2 pounds ground beef
1 pound lean pork
1¼ cups unseasoned bread
   crumbs (preferably homemade)
1 finely grated medium onion
1 teaspoon salt
½ teaspoon fresh ground black
   pepper

1 teaspoon nutmeg
2 eggs (room temperature)
Milk
2 tablespoons flour
Butter

Grind beef and pork together and set aside. In a large mixing bowl combine the bread crumbs, onion, salt, pepper, nutmeg, and eggs. Mix together well (best technique is to use your hands) and add enough milk to make the mixture gloppy. Add ground meat to this mixture, which should become stiff and sticky.

Form meatballs (keep small if using for appetizers) but do not overwork the meat or meatballs will be tough. Brown in butter and drain meatballs on paper towels. Save 2 tablespoons of fat in skillet to make gravy. Add 1 cup of hot water and scrape drippings from skillet, mixing with the water. Add salt and pepper to taste and keep on low heat. In a shaker, mix ½ cup milk and 2 tablespoons of flour until smooth. Add to pan of drippings and stir constantly until thick. Put meatballs in casserole, pour gravy over meatballs, and heat covered for 45 minutes in a 325° oven. After cooking is over, meatballs and gravy can be frozen.

Estelle Parsons

Stage and screen actress

*A*cademy Award winner Estelle Parsons was born in Lynn, Massachusetts, and lived in Marblehead, until she left for New York City, where she has resided ever since.

"We always summered in Wolfeboro, New Hampshire. My family still summers there. I graduated from Oak Grove School for Girls, Vassalboro, Maine, and Connecticut College for Women, New London, Connecticut, and attended Boston University Law School and the New England Conservatory of Music. The Parsons family dates back to 1632 in Northampton, Massachusetts. I believe I am the first member of the family to settle outside New England — in a foreign country: New York City. On my mother's side, pure Swedish.

"I am currently doing *A Sense of Humor,* a play by Ernest Thompson who is from Oakland, Maine, and in it with me is Jack Lemmon who is from Boston and Wolfeboro, New Hampshire. Small world."

SWEDISH PULT

"My favorite for a cold winter morning is Swedish Pult, which my Swedish mother introduced to my New England father. We did not have it often and so we looked forward to it with great enthusiasm. It made a family occasion. It is a dish indigenous to the far north of Sweden, the land of the midnight sun, where my mother was born. My grandfather (before I was born) used to pay my grandmother $5 every time she made it because it took so much time and was a messy job. Today it might be easy with a Cuisinart. I don't know. I don't have one.

"Sometimes it is eaten hot, sliced and spread with butter, but usually it is cooled, sliced, and fried slowly in butter in a skillet until light brown. Then spread it with butter and with a glass of milk you have a wonderful hearty meal. Pult eating contests are one of the happiest memories of my childhood."

4 large raw potatoes
1 to 2 pounds beef liver
2½ cups rye flour
2½ cups white flour

1 tablespoon salt
2 cups cold water (about)
½ pound salt pork, diced

Put potatoes and liver through food chopper. Add all ingredients except salt pork in large bowl. Dough should be firm enough to make balls 3 inches in diameter. Put a few diced pork pieces in center of each ball. Drop balls into boiling salted water and boil slowly for about an hour.

ESTELLE PARSONS' WALNUT TORTE

"Estelle Parsons' Walnut Torte was created because my two daughters, Abbie and Martha Gehman, had a high school graduation party and there were nuts galore left over — to eat, not the human kind. This recipe was a way to use up the walnuts. I made it for the March of Dimes Gourmet Gala at the Waldorf-Astoria and won first prize for desserts."

CAKE

2½ cups ground walnuts
¾ cup sugar

7 egg whites

Mix together walnuts and sugar. Beat egg whites until stiff. Fold in walnut and sugar mixture. Divide into 3 round cake tins (8 or 9 inches) which have been well buttered and floured. Bake 15 or 20 minutes or until delicately browned in 400° oven. Cool in tins.

FILLING

3 egg yolks
3 tablespoons very strong coffee
½ cup sugar

½ cup chopped walnuts
1 tablespoon sugar
Confectioners sugar

Mix egg yolks, coffee, and sugar and heat over low flame, stirring briskly until thick and creamy. Do not boil. Cool.

Stir chopped walnuts and sugar over low flame until browned. Add to cooled coffee and egg mixture. Spread filling between cake layers. Sprinkle top of cake with confectioners sugar.

Noel Perrin

Writer, professor, and farmer

Born in New York City, Noel Perrin has been teaching at Dartmouth College for the last 25 years, and doing part-time farming in Vermont for about 20. ("I have a prior connection with New England in that my mother's family came to Massachusetts Bay in the 1630s.") He has written three books of essays about life on a part-time farm called *First Person Rural*, *Second Person Rural*, and *Third Person Rural*, and a book about maple sugaring called *Amateur Sugar Maker*.

RED FLANNEL HASH

"I first encountered this noble winter dish at a supper put on by the Timothy Frost Methodist Church in Thetford Center [Vermont] and I understand its original function was to use up leftovers from a New England boiled dinner. This recipe is consequently quite flexible.

"In its simplest form, however, you use equal amounts of boiled corned beef and boiled potatoes, and a slightly smaller quantity of cooked beets. You put everything through a meat grinder, and then heat it in a cast-iron skillet into which you have first put a little bacon grease.

"A couple of helpings of red flannel hash, and you are ready to face twenty-below weather with equanimity."

Vermont Baklava

"This is my own recipe — if you can dignify the instructions with the name 'recipe.' They're not complicated. All you do is set your toaster on medium, toast a couple of slices of good quality white bread (the cheap air-filled stuff won't do), and put them on a plate. Then you pour a generous quantity of medium or dark amber maple syrup over them. (These were Vermont grades A and B before the U.S. Government pre-empted maple grading.) Next you wait a couple of minutes for it to soak in. Then you eat the toast. For some reason this combination yields a buttery as well as a maple-y flavor; it's good stuff.

"I happened on it soon after I began to sell maple syrup commercially. People would stop by to buy some. I'd ask them what grade they wanted, and often enough they were unaware there were grades. So, I'd give them samples. You need a vehicle for the syrup — it's too intense just in a spoon. There was not always time to make a batch of pancakes. Before I knew it, I was serving Vermont baklava."

William Pierce

Broadcaster

William Pierce was born in New Bedford, Massachusetts, and is a member of the Mayflower Descendants via William White, signer of the *Mayflower Compact*. "The first William Pierce (spelled Piers in English maritime history) came to America as the master of the *Queen Anne* and the second voyage of the *Mayflower*, etc. I was educated in the public schools of New Bedford and at Hebron Academy and Bowdoin College, both in Maine. My home is in Hingham, Massachusetts. I have had the happy job of announcing the broadcasts of the Boston Symphony and Boston Pops Orchestra for 31 years."

HERBED CREAM CHEESE

"When Boursin became somewhat expensive, my sister, Rachel Coburn, who is much smarter than I, dreamed up this substitute."

8 ounces cream cheese	½ cup heavy cream
2 garlic cloves, put through garlic press	1 tablespoon fines herbes
	½ teaspoon salt

Mix thoroughly and chill overnight. Use as spread for crackers. Also good used as spread on pumpernickel bread for cold roast beef sandwiches.

TUNA TERRINE

"The top of this mixture can be gussied up with sliced black olives, etc. before adding the consommé."

1 can (7 ounces) of tuna in oil
3 tablespoons cognac
2 hard-cooked eggs
6 ounces cream cheese
Salt and pepper
Canned consommé (chilled
  almost to jelled state)

Combine all but consommé in work bowl with steel blade until very smooth. Spoon into 1½- or 2-cup mold from which it can be served. Smooth top with spatula. Cover with semi-jelled consommé. Chill until firm. Serve with toast points or crackers.

FISH CASSEROLE SAUCE

"This is a marvelous sauce for any fish casserole. These are the ingredients as I use them. Each individual will want to change something probably. That's part of the fun of cooking."

4 tablespoons butter
4 tablespoons flour
2 cups whole milk (perhaps some
  heavy cream for part of it)
1 teaspoon salt
⅛ teaspoon pepper
½ teaspoon celery salt
1 egg yolk (remove from heat to
  add beaten egg yolk)
2 tablespoons dry sherry (or
  vermouth)
1 tablespoon minced onion
1 tablespoon minced parsley
Dash of cayenne pepper
Drained canned mushrooms to
  taste

Cook roux for 2-3 minutes, then add ingredients as listed, one at a time. Mix in whatever fish you are using (i.e., quart of lobster meat, scallops, etc.) and pour into casserole. To stretch, 1 cup of soft bread crumbs or a can of crab meat can be added. If desired, sprinkle crumbs and cheese on top. Bake at 400° until it bubbles (25 or more minutes). For individual casseroles, 15-20 minutes.

Lee Remick

Actress

*L*ee Remick has appeared on Broadway, in over 20 motion pictures, and in various television productions. She is married to film producer William "Kip" Gowans, who hails from England. They both have two children from previous marriages. "I was born in Boston and now spend my summers on the Cape after having spent many childhood summers there. Currently, I 'commute' between the Cape and Los Angeles."

LEE REMICK'S SEAFOOD MARINARA

2 pounds fresh fish or shellfish
(halibut, swordfish, corbina,
bass, snapper, lobster meat,
scallops, or peeled and
deveined raw shrimp)
2 tablespoons olive oil
1 medium onion, chopped
2 or 3 garlic cloves, crushed

¾ teaspoon salt
1 tablespoon soft bread crumbs
1 small tomato, peeled and
chopped
¼ to ½ cup minced parsley
½ cup dry sherry
½ cup water

Sauté the fish or shellfish in olive oil over moderate heat, just until delicately browned. As soon as fish has started to brown, add onion, garlic, salt, and crumbs. Cook about 1 minute. Add chopped tomato and parsley. Lower heat and simmer 3 minutes. Add sherry and water; simmer uncovered 3 minutes longer. They'll rave!

Serves 4-6 as an entrée, 15 as an hors d'oeuvre.

Elliot Richardson

Lawyer and government official

Born in Boston and educated at Harvard, Elliot Richardson has served in numerous public offices. He was lieutenant governor of Massachusetts (1965-67) and the state's attorney general (1967-69). At the federal level his appointments include secretary of state, secretary of health, education, and welfare, secretary of defense, secretary of commerce, attorney general of the United States, and ambassador to the Court of St. James. He is currently a senior resident partner in the law firm Milbank, Tweed, Hadley, and McCloy, and resides in the Washington, D.C., area.

SYLVIA'S CAKE

A Brookline, Massachusetts, friend of the Richardsons is the source for this recipe. The cake is delicious in either version, frosted or plain.

*1 box Duncan Hines yellow cake mix (or chocolate)
*1 box instant lemon pudding mix (or chocolate)
4 eggs, room temperature
½ pint sour cream, room temperature
½ cup vegetable oil
*Lemon and orange rind, grated (omit with chocolate recipe)
*1 teaspoon Grand Marnier (or 1 teaspoon powdered instant coffee)
Pinch of mace

Mix with electric mixer at #4 speed for *7 minutes*. Bake in greased angel cake pan at 350° for 1 hour. Cool in pan, right side up. Dust with powdered sugar when cool.

*If chocolate flavor is preferred, the changes listed above may be substituted.

Continued

Elliot Richardson *continued*

CAPE COD CRANBERRY NUT BREAD

The Richardsons associate this with visits to eastern Cape Cod and a friend there who, some years ago, gave them a loaf of the bread and the recipe. They now have it on all festive occasions: Thanksgiving, Christmas, weddings, birthdays, etc.

1 cup whole raw cranberries	1½ teaspoons baking powder
1 cup chopped walnuts	½ teaspoon soda
1 tablespoon flour	2 eggs, slightly beaten
2 cups flour	2 tablespoons melted shortening
1 cup sugar	¾ cup orange juice
½ teaspoon salt	Grated rind of 1 orange

Dredge cranberries and nuts in 1 tablespoon flour; set aside. Sift dry ingredients together. Combine eggs, shortening, juice, and orange rind in measuring cup. Add water if necessary to make one cup liquid; stir into dry ingredients until well mixed. Fold in cranberry nut mixture. Bake in greased loaf pan for 1 hour at 350° (check at 45 minutes to see if done: top springs back when poked; toothpick inserted comes out clean). Cool on rack, wrap in foil, and store in refrigerator. Very good slightly toasted as well as just sliced.

Bill Rodgers

Marathon runner

Bill Rodgers has spent his whole life in New England. Born in Hartford, he grew up in Newington, Connecticut, graduated from Wesleyan University, and currently lives in Sherborn, Massachusetts. Bill was a member of the 1976 U.S. Olympic Team and is co-author with Joe Concannon of *Marathoning*. Because he runs between 120 and 140 miles a week, he can eat just about any quantity of anything he wishes — and does!

CHICKEN DIVAN

Bill's number one favorite dish. Although this makes enough for eight servings, it is said that he can eat the whole thing himself.

2 packages (10 ounces each) frozen broccoli
2 cups cooked chicken (approximately 4 chicken breasts)
2 cans cream of chicken soup
2 tablespoons lemon juice
1 cup mayonnaise
1 teaspoon curry powder
1 to 2 cups shredded cheddar cheese
¾ cup bread crumbs
4 tablespoons butter

Partially cook and drain the broccoli. Arrange in bottom of buttered 13″ x 9″ pan. Place slices of chicken over broccoli. Combine soup, lemon juice, mayonnaise, and curry and blend well. Pour over chicken, sprinkle with cheese, and top with crumbs that have been mixed with butter. Bake 30 minutes at 350°.   *Serves 8.*

Continued

Bill Rodgers *continued*

NORWEGIAN SARDINE SPREAD

Runner magazine once did an analysis of Bill's diet and found that a lot of his eating is more like snacking. He enjoys this for lunch with crackers. It's also tasty as a sandwich spread or vegetable dip.

2 cans (3¾ ounces each) Norway sardines in oil, drained
2 tablespoons butter or margarine, softened
2 tablespoons lime or lemon juice
1 tablespoon drained capers
¼ cup chopped parsley
Pepper

In an electric blender, combine sardines, butter, lime juice, and capers. Blend, turning on and off, until smooth, scraping sides of container as needed. Remove to bowl; stir in parsley and pepper to taste. Chill 1 hour. Spoon into crock. Garnish with additional sardines and chopped parsley, if desired. Serve with assorted crackers and bread. *Makes 1 cup.*

HUMMINGBIRD CAKE

This recipe was obtained from a 70-year-old runner at the Iroquois Hill Climb in Louisville, Kentucky.

3 cups all-purpose flour
2 cups sugar
1 teaspoon salt
1 teaspoon soda
1 teaspoon ground cinnamon
3 eggs, beaten
1½ cups salad oil
1½ teaspoons vanilla
1 can (8 ounces) crushed pineapple, undrained
2 cups chopped pecans or walnuts, divided
2 cups chopped bananas
Cream cheese frosting (your favorite recipe)

Combine dry ingredients in a large mixing bowl; add eggs and salad oil, stirring until dry ingredients are moistened. Do not beat. Stir in vanilla, pineapple, 1 cup chopped nuts, and the bananas. Spoon batter into 3 well-greased and floured 9-inch cake pans. Bake at 350° for 25-30 minutes, or until cake tests done. Cool in pans 10 minutes; remove from pans and cool completely. Spread frosting between layers and on top and sides of cake and sprinkle with remaining cup of nuts.

S-W

*Clockwise from top: Tom Winship, Benjamin Spock,
John Williams, Margaret Chase Smith*

Arthur M. Schlesinger, Jr.

Writer and educator

*A*rthur Schlesinger attended public schools in Cambridge and Phillips Exeter Academy in New Hampshire. A graduate of Harvard University (Class of '38), he also taught history there for a number of years, as did his father. Mr. Schlesinger has authored, co-authored, or edited over 30 books and has received two Pulitzer Prizes (for *The Age of Jackson* and *A Thousand Days*) and two National Book Awards (for *A Thousand Days* and *Robert Kennedy and His Times*). Mr. Schlesinger has six children and lives in Manhattan, with his wife, Alexandra.

"Though born in Ohio, I lived in New England (Cambridge, Massachusetts) from 1924 to 1942 and from 1947 to 1961, summered for many years in the 1920s and 1930s and again in the 1950s on Cape Cod (and, most recently, on Martha's Vineyard) and still, though a New York City resident for more than 15 years, consider myself a New Englander at heart."

BUTTERFLIED LAMB WITH TARRAGON GRILLED OVER CHARCOAL

"This is an adaptation of a recipe of Pierre Franey's that I greatly enjoy cooking as well as eating."

Have the butcher "butterfly" — i.e., debone, open up, and trim — a 7-8 pound leg of lamb. Put ¼ cup of oil in a baking dish, and lay the lamb out flat in the oil. Sprinkle the lamb on both sides with chopped tarragon (at least 3 tablespoons), garlic (1 tablespoon), ¼ cup tarragon vinegar, Dijon mustard, butter, and freshly ground pepper. Turn and rub the lamb so that it is evenly coated by the marinade. Soak the lamb for several hours.

Cooking: Place the lamb flat on the charcoal grill, and cook each side 8-10 minutes. When cooking is done (this lamb is best served rare), put the lamb back in the marinating dish and allow to rest for 15 minutes or so in the marinade before carving. Serve the meat with the pan liquid.   *Serves 6-8.*

Eric Sloane

Artist and author

World-renowned as an author, artist, and meteorologist, Eric Sloane has executed murals for the Air and Space Museum in Washington, established the Eric Sloane Museum of Early American Tools in Kent, Connecticut, and has written and illustrated many books, including *Seasons of American Past, Age of Barns, Diary of an Early American Boy, Reverence for Wood,* and *School Days: Early Americana — Little Red School House.* Mr. Sloane, who spent 30 years in Connecticut, now lives in Santa Fe, New Mexico.

SLOANE'S PEAR FONDUE

"Once while serving fondue (hot cheese sauce on toasted bread) I ran out of bread. Having a number of fresh pears, I cut them into slices to use instead of breadsticks. Pear and cheese make a gourmet combination and so Sloane's Pear Fondue was invented."

HOLLOW-WEENIES

"One Halloween, dinner consisted of hot dogs and beans. By hollowing out some of the meat and stuffing the hot dogs with the beans, I had Hollow-weenies!"

OATMEAL FLAPJACKS

"When preparing oatmeal for breakfast, I always double the amount and save the leftover for tomorrow's Oatmeal Flapjacks with maple syrup — an ideal winter breakfast with coffee."

Margaret Chase Smith

Former member of Congress and nationally syndicated columnist

The recipient of numerous awards and 85 honorary degrees, Margaret Chase Smith has spent most of her long and productive life involved in local, state, and national government. A native of Skowhegan, Maine, she has the distinction of being the only woman elected to serve in both houses of Congress, and the first whose name was placed in nomination for the presidency by a major party (at the 1964 Republican Convention). In 1973 Mrs. Smith began a new career — that of visiting professor and lecturer at various colleges and universities across the country.

"Here are recipes that I have used most often. I have cooked throughout my life, less during my 36 years at the U.S. Capitol."

BLUEBERRY MUFFINS

1 egg	2 cups flour
⅔ cup sugar	½ teaspoon salt
2 tablespoons melted butter	2 teaspoons baking powder
1 cup sweet milk	1½ cups blueberries

Mix in order given. Flour blueberries well. Bake in greased muffin tins in hot oven (400°) for 25 minutes.

BAKED BEANS

1 quart dry beans
¼ teaspoon soda
3 tablespoons olive oil
Small square of salt pork
2 teaspoons salt

½ teaspoon ginger
Pinch of mustard
Pinch of red pepper
1 tablespoon molasses
1 peeled onion

Soak beans overnight. Drain off water through strainer. Cover with cold water to which soda has been added. Parboil until the skin of the beans breaks, not too much. Let set a few minutes, then drain off water. Rinse with cold water. Add olive oil, salt pork, salt, ginger, mustard, red pepper, molasses, and onion. Cover with hot water. Let stand on top of warm stove a few minutes. Place in oven and bake slowly for 8 hours, keeping covered with water as needed.

Benjamin Spock

Physician, educator, and writer

Dr. Spock was born in New Haven, Connecticut, graduated from Phillips Academy (Andover) and Yale College, and spent two years at Yale Medical School before transferring to Columbia University. Author of the classic *Common Sense Book of Baby and Child Care,* he has written or collaborated on many other books, with topics ranging from child care to politics.

"Since retirement I've been on the road every other month, speaking mainly at universities, for the benefit of peace groups and the Peoples Party, whose presidential candidate I was in 1972 and whose vice presidential candidate I was in 1976, most often on the topic of the need for radical political action but also on child development. During the alternate months I sail a boat in Maine or the Virgin Islands."

OATMEAL

This is Dr. Spock's favorite recipe, which he cooks and eats everyday.

2 cups water	Dash of salt
½ cup steel-cut oats	

Cook slowly for 30 minutes. Serve with cream and maple syrup.

Paul Szep

Editorial cartoonist

Recipient of the Pulitzer Prize in 1974 and 1977, Paul Szep has lived in the Boston area since 1967, when he went to work for *The Boston Globe* as editorial cartoonist. Prior to that he was sports cartoonist for the *Hamilton Spectator* in Hamilton, Ontario, Canada, where he was born, and then graphics designer at the *Financial Post* in Toronto. Mr. Szep currently resides in Brookline, Massachusetts, and spends most summers on Martha's Vineyard or Nantucket.

SZEP'S BROCCOLI

"This was prepared at the Second Annual Gourmet Gala for the March of Dimes. It was a special evening, a lot of fun for a really good cause."

1 large head of broccoli	A bunch of scallions, chopped
½ pound prosciutto, cut into 2-inch pieces	Thyme
	Salt and pepper
½ pound Montrechet goat cheese or similar soft goat cheese, sliced	½ cup spicy V-8 juice
	½ cup canned chicken stock
3 large tomatoes, peeled, seeded, and chopped	

Cut broccoli and blanch until tender. Drain well and place in casserole dish. Arrange prosciutto and cheese over broccoli. Sprinkle with tomatoes, scallions, thyme, and salt and pepper. Mix liquids together and pour over casserole. Bake at 350° for about 20 minutes, or until cheese is melted and bubbly.

Continued

Paul Szep *continued*

RASPBERRY DELIGHT PIE

"This recipe is handed down from my mother's family in Canada. It was especially nice in the summer."

CRUST
 1 package of vanilla wafers
 5 tablespoons butter

Crush wafers and mix with butter. Pat into square pan. Let stand in refrigerator 20 minutes.

FILLING
 1 large package marshmallows
 ½ cup milk
 1 package (9 ounces) frozen
   raspberries, thawed
 ½ pint whipping cream
 1 tablespoon cornstarch

Combine marshmallows and milk in saucepan and heat until melted. Drain raspberries, saving juice. Whip cream until stiff. Fold in berries and cooled marshmallow mixture. Spoon into prepared pan. Add cornstarch to reserved juice and heat until mixture clears. Drizzle on top of pie. Refrigerate a few hours before serving.

STOUFFER'S LASAGNA

"This has become a joke among my friends. Over the years I have at least once fooled each of them into thinking I was a closet Italian.

"Purchase in supermarket, take home, remove from package. Place in preheated oven at 400°, leave in one hour and fifteen minutes, remove and place in large tin plate. Serve at dinner party and tell friends how you slaved all day preparing it."

William O. Taylor

Newspaper executive

Chairman of the board and publisher of *The Boston Globe,* William Taylor was born in Boston and attended St. Paul's School (Concord, New Hampshire) and Harvard (Class of '54). He has worked for the *Globe* since 1956. His wife, Sally Coxe Taylor, volunteers at Massachusetts General Hospital and is one of the Lawrence Winship Book Award judges. The Taylors have three sons (one working, one in college, one in boarding school) and three dogs — two Norfolk terriers and a golden retriever.

CUCUMBER SOUP

"This soup is a combination of a number of other recipes. It is very popular with family and friends."

4 small cucumbers	Dill weed
1 large onion, quartered	Worcestershire sauce
1 large garlic clove	Tabasco
1 can condensed potato soup	Chives
2 cups (at least) chicken broth (preferably homemade)	

Peel and slice 3 cucumbers; slice 1 unpeeled. In a blender or food processor, chop cucumbers, onion, and garlic in batches. Pour in bowl. Purée potato soup and add to bowl. Add chicken broth to desired consistency. Chill and add remaining ingredients to taste.

Continued

William Taylor *continued*

MRS. THOMPSON'S CAKE

"This recipe, for our family birthday cake, is from a baby nurse we had for our third son."

1 yellow cake mix	Grated rind of 1 lemon
4 eggs	½ cup orange juice
¾ cup water	¼ cup rum
¾ cup oil	1¼ cups confectioners sugar

Combine cake mix, eggs, water, and oil, and beat for 5 minutes. Fold in grated lemon rind. Pour into greased and floured 13″ x 9″ Pyrex pan. Bake at 350° for 30-35 minutes.

Meanwhile, mix orange juice, rum, and confectioners sugar. When cake is done, prick top with fork and spoon orange juice mixture on top and down sides until saturated. When cool, cover with foil. It will keep moist for as long as it lasts.

Rob Trowbridge

Publishing executive

President of Yankee Publishing Incorporated and publisher of *The Old Farmer's Almanac* and *Yankee* magazine, Rob Trowbridge was born in Salem, Massachusetts, raised in and around Boston, and educated at Phillips Exeter Academy and Princeton. During his 20 years in publishing, he has also served six terms as a member of the New Hampshire General Court, three terms in the House of Representatives, and three as a state senator. An avid sailor and enthusiastic musician (banjoist with a local jazz band), Mr. Trowbridge lives in Dublin, New Hampshire, with his wife, Lorna, and their four children.

MY MOTHER'S GOULASH

"This recipe came from a Mrs. St. John, who was a parishioner of my father's in Morristown, New Jersey. My mother, however, was the one to recognize its ability to feed endless amounts of people without too much expense, and I associate the dish with the end-of-summer parties we would throw in our barn in Chesham, New Hampshire. She had a great big Garland stove that could cook for mobs, and this recipe allowed her to cook ahead and then just warm it up at the time when everyone was arriving. Many a song was sung over this goulash; my father never subscribed to the idea that one should not sing at the table — in fact he carried the opposite thought to the extreme, and most of our parties were one continual "burst" of singing from someone. So, when you are cutting celery and frying the hamburger, sing a little ditty; it goes with it!"

1½ pounds hamburg	1 large can tomatoes
Small bunch celery	Salt and pepper to taste
3 green peppers	1 package spaghetti
Butter	Grated cheese

Cook hamburg, celery, and peppers (cut finely) in plenty of butter. When hamburg is done, add tomatoes. Season well with salt and pepper, and simmer slowly while spaghetti is cooking. Add spaghetti and simmer 5 minutes. Sprinkle with grated cheese. Even better reheated.   *Serves 10.*

Continued

Rob Trowbridge *continued*

CLAM LINGUINE

"This recipe was taught to me by a fellow sailor, Betsy Harris, now of Dublin, New Hampshire, but then just having returned from Europe where she and her husband, John, had been cruising for more than nine months. Once when I was visiting them informally she all of a sudden said, 'Why don't we have dinner?', and proceeded to tell me that when she wants to cook something on board that looks fancy but really is within the reach of most galleys, this is her answer. Not only did I enjoy the meal greatly but I learned to make the clam sauce myself. It remains to this day the only meal cooked by me that my crew will eat (my concoction of stewed tomatoes mixed can for can with petit pois, known as 'sloppy,' has not been universally accepted). Canned clams are readily available and easy to store; the only thing you have to keep track of is the olive oil — real olive oil makes a difference."

16 ounces linguine	½ teaspoon oregano
⅓ cup olive oil	2 cans (7½ ounces each) minced
¼ cup butter	clams, drained (reserve liquid)
3 cloves garlic, minced	3 tablespoons chopped parsley
½ teaspoon salt	½ cup grated Parmesan cheese
1 teaspoon freshly ground pepper	(optional)
½ teaspoon basil	

Cook linguine according to package directions. Drain well. Meanwhile, heat oil and butter in a porcelain or enameled iron saucepan. Add garlic and sauté gently 2 minutes (do not brown). Add salt, pepper, basil, oregano, and reserved clam liquid. Simmer 2 to 3 minutes. Add clams to the sauce and heat well. Add parsley. Pour clam sauce over hot, well-drained pasta and mix gently. Sprinkle with cheese, if desired. *Serves 4-6.*

Paul Tsongas

U.S. senator

Senator Paul Tsongas was born and raised in Lowell, Massachusetts. A graduate of Dartmouth College, he spent two years in Ethiopia in the Peace Corps before entering Yale Law School. He has served as Lowell city councillor, U.S. representative, and since 1979, U.S. senator. Author of *The Road from Here: Liberalism and Realities in the 1980s,* Senator Tsongas lives in Lowell with his wife, Niki, and their three daughters.

NIKI TSONGAS' APPLE CAKE

1½ cups oil
2 cups sugar
3 eggs
3 cups flour
1 teaspoon salt
1 teaspoon cinnamon
1 teaspoon baking soda
1 teaspoon vanilla

5 cups peeled, cored, and thickly sliced apples (Delicious work best)
1 cup chopped walnuts
1 cup raisins (optional)
1 teaspoon lemon zest (or grated lemon peel)

Preheat oven to 350°. Beat oil and sugar together. Add eggs and beat until mixture is creamy. Sift together flour, salt, cinnamon, and baking soda. Stir into batter. Then add vanilla, apples, walnuts, raisins, and lemon peel and stir to blend. Turn mixture into a buttered and floured 9″ angel food tube pan. Bake for 1 hour, 15 minutes or until done. Cool in the pan before turning out. Serve with ice cream or whipped cream. *Serves 8-10.*

Violette Verdy

Ballerina and artistic director

French-born, classically trained ballerina, Violette Verdy performed with scores of internationally ranked ballet companies during her career as a dancer, including the Ballet de Paris de Roland Petit, the Royal Ballet, London Festival Ballet, and American Ballet Theatre. She was a member of George Ballanchine's New York City Ballet from 1958 to 1976 and then retired from the stage to direct the Paris Opera Ballet, becoming the first woman to hold that position. Three years later Miss Verdy joined The Boston Ballet, where she continues to serve as artistic director.

VEALETTE'S PÂTÉ

1 pound veal steak
1 pound pork breast
1 shallot, finely chopped
1 clove garlic, minced
¾ teaspoon salt

¼ teaspoon pepper
Bouquet garni: 2 sprigs parsley, ½ bay leaf, ¼ teaspoon thyme wrapped in cheesecloth and tied with string

Have the butcher grind the meat coarsely. Add shallot, garlic, salt, and pepper; mix well and pack into a pâté mold, rounding the top so that the fat will collect on the sides during cooking. Lay bouquet garni on side of mold and bake at 375° for 1 hour. Test with a knife. If done, knife will come out clean. Unmold and serve cold.

Serves 6.

Robert Vickrey

Artist

Robert Vickrey's work has appeared on over 75 *Time* magazine covers, as well as in *American Artist, Architectural Digest,* and *Yankee* magazine, among others. His paintings have been exhibited throughout the United States, including in the Metropolitan Museum, the Corcoran Gallery of Art, the National Collection of Fine Arts, and the Butler Institute of American Art. Mr. Vickrey is a graduate of Yale and Wesleyan Universities and Yale School of Fine Arts.

"I started coming to Cape Cod 32 years ago and have come here every summer until ten years ago when my wife, Marjorie, and I moved to the Cape full-time. We now live in Orleans."

POT ROAST ROBERT

"For many years I cooked for myself and became a passable cook, but I never enjoyed cooking. My wife, who is an excellent cook, planned a dinner party. She departed for Boston that morning intending to return shortly. She called in a panic saying she would be tied up all day and would I please whip up something for dinner. We had a pot roast in the refrigerator. I rushed down from my studio, put the pot roast in a pot, and improvised, making up the following recipe as I went along. Everyone, including myself, was amazed at how good it was. Occasionally I am called upon for a repeat performance."

6-pound pot roast
2 cans Progresso Lentil Soup (20-ounce size)
24 ounces sour cream
2 cups burgundy
1 medium-size can potatoes
All leftover vegetables you may have lying around

Immerse roast in water and bring to a boil. Simmer five hours. If water has not evaporated, take some out and leave about ¼ pot of water with the roast. Add the soup, sour cream, burgundy, canned potatoes, and vegetables. Simmer another half hour or so.

Ulrike Welsch

Photographer

*U*ntil she moved to New England from her native Germany in 1964, Ulrike Welsch considered photography to be only a hobby. In this country, however, she became a professional and in 1966 was hired as a staff photographer for the *Boston Herald Traveler;* from there she moved to *The Boston Globe,* where she spent nine years. In addition to teaching photojournalism, Ms. Welsch has also contributed to various publications, including *Life, Time,* and *Yankee,* and has had two books published: *The World I Love to See* and *Faces of New England.*

POTATO PANCAKES

"The pancakes taste best and crispy when they are eaten out of the pan!!! Sit down and eat with applesauce (it balances the rich pancakes well!) or if you feel like splurging on richness, sour cream is delicious also! Sit and eat while the next pair is sizzling in the pan. Adjust the heat to your appetite. If you are a fast eater, keep the heat up; if you eat slowly, turn the heat down! A good beer tastes very fine with it."

5 or 6 medium-size potatoes (about 3 pounds)	2 tablespoons flour
1 large onion	Salt
2 eggs	Pepper

Peel and grate potatoes. (For grating, use potato ricer, which is best, or a hand grater; an Osterizer works on chop or grate, but is a little tricky to manage. Best when potatoes are dry. It makes a kind of purée. Use more potatoes.) During ricing, grate onion sections in between. Onion prevents potatoes from turning brown. Stir occasionally to mix onion under while grating the remaining potatoes. Potatoes have lots of water. Pour water out, or put into a sieve to drain. Then add eggs, flour, and salt and pepper to taste. (I use seven pinches of salt.) Mix well. Use good nonsticking pan (8-inch bottom) and plenty of oil. When pan is very hot and oil sizzling, scoop in about 2 big spoonfuls of batter for each pancake half. Pack a little, shape a little. If pancake does not move freely, loosen up with spatula and from then on only push around with pan-handle. When edges turn crisp-golden brown, check bottomside. If crispy, golden brown also, turn over.

Makes 6 half pan-size servings.

Lael Wertenbaker

Writer

Lael Wertenbaker grew up in the South, left for New York City when she was 18, became a reporter for Time Inc., then a foreign and war correspondent, and lived in France with her husband Charles Wertenbaker. After his death, she went back to New York, where she remained until her children were grown. Having spent some time at the MacDowell Colony in Peterborough, New Hampshire, Mrs. Wertenbaker was familiar with the Monadnock Region and decided to move there. "The mountains were very like the low Pyrenees of southwestern France, the pine woods and mud reminiscent of childhood in Alabama and Louisiana, and having covered as a reporter the U.S. House of Representatives, the Houses of Parliament, and the Chambre des Députés, the town meetings far more exciting and truly participatory." She has lived in Nelson, New Hampshire, for close to twenty years.

CHICKEN COOKED IN A CHINESE CLAY POT

"Chicken cooked this way tastes good, stays moist, and can be prepared in advance and baked without any attention. Warning: Take care not to burn your hands when removing from the oven and taking off the cover."

"Stuff chicken with any favorite dressing. Mine is bread crumbs with chopped onion, liver, peppers, which have been sautéed, plus chopped celery. Rub chicken with oil or melted butter and salt and pepper to taste. Place in pot which has been previously soaked in water to prevent cracking and thoroughly wiped dry. Bake in oven at 500° for 90 minutes."

John Williams

Composer and conductor

Recipient of Grammy, Emmy, and Academy awards, composer John Williams has been conductor of the Boston Pops since 1980. Born of New England parents (his mother is from Boston, his father from Maine), Mr. Williams spends time on the East and West Coasts. He has written the scores for numerous motion pictures, including *Close Encounters of the Third Kind, Dracula, Superman, Jaws, Star Wars, Raiders of the Lost Ark,* and, most recently, *Indiana Jones in the Temple of Doom.*

PEPPER STEAK DIJON

"This recipe is from a favorite country French restaurant in Los Angeles called Au Petit Cafe, which always has the waiters recite the menus, including ingredients. 'All' we had to do was work out the proportions, which took a long time!"

Cracked pepper	⅓ cup half and half
2 filets	1 tablespoon Dijon mustard
1 tablespoon butter	½ teaspoon Marsala wine
2 tablespoons brandy	Pinch of nutmeg

Press cracked pepper into both sides of 2 filets. Sauté to preferred degree of doneness in butter. Remove steaks and keep warm. To drippings in pan add brandy and flame. When flames have subsided, add half and half, Dijon mustard, Marsala wine, and nutmeg to pan. Let reduce a bit and pour over steaks. Serve immediately.

Serves 2.

BANANA NUT CAKE

"This recipe has been handed down for three generations. It was always the cake requested on birthdays."

CAKE

½ cup butter
1⅓ cups sugar
2 eggs, beaten
1½ cups mashed very ripe
  bananas
2 cups flour
1 teaspoon baking powder
¾ teaspoon salt
1 teaspoon soda
1 cup sour cream
1 cup chopped walnuts
1 teaspoon vanilla

Cream butter and sugar. Add beaten eggs and mashed bananas. Sift flour with baking powder, salt, and soda. Add to egg mixture alternately with sour cream. Fold in nuts and vanilla. Pour batter into two 8″ or 9″ buttered and floured cake pans. Bake at 325° for approximately 30 minutes or until cake tests done. Cool. Ice with coffee icing.

ICING

4 cups sifted powdered sugar
6 tablespoons soft butter
½ teaspoon salt
4 tablespoons strong coffee

Mix all ingredients together and ice cooled cake layers. Garnish with whole walnuts if desired.

Serves 8.

Thomas Winship

Journalist and editor

*E*ditor of *The Boston Globe,* Thomas Winship was born in Mt. Auburn Hospital in Cambridge, Massachusetts, and spent the first 20 years of his life in South Sudbury, Massachusetts. "After a 13-year stint working on *The Washington Post* and *The Boston Globe* in Washington, D.C., I returned to Boston and have lived ever so happily in Lincoln, Massachusetts, since 1959. I spend my vacation time in Randolph, Vermont. I returned to New England largely because I have a massive love affair with the turf of Boston and New England. I travel the area extensively year in and year out.

"I do not want to leave the impression that I am the full-time cook of my household. I am blessed with a wife, who, after a 12-hour working day in her own profession, gets tremendous joy out of improvising memorable meals seven days a week. [Elizabeth Winship writes the "Ask Beth" column for the *Globe.*] Everything she cooks has a little surprise; is a work of art. That is not baloney. It is the truth."

CAPE COD TURKEY DINNER

"This is a fine dish, a complete meal in itself and a tight budgeteer's dream. It came down through my father's family, who never had a dime to spare."

Boiled carrots	Salted codfish
Boiled beets	Pork scraps
Boiled potatoes, without their jackets	White sauce, with cut-up boiled eggs

"The technique of preparing the cooked food for a Cape Cod Turkey Dinner is the most important aspect of the meal, according to Winship tradition. The various ingredients are placed on the plate and each one is cut up as fine as possible with a knife and fork. Mashing the vegetables is verboten. The din of five or six people cutting away at their carrots, beets, and potatoes individually forecloses comfortable conversation.

"The game is to cut up all the ingredients as fine as possible. Once they are mixed together, sprinkle on the fried pork scraps. Then the egg sauce is poured over the massive mound of the above. Enjoy it!"

OYSTER STEW

"This is another Winship tradition for Christmas Eve. It's oyster stew and, if necessary, can be made in ten minutes. Preferably, make it a day ahead of time for mellowing. It is all you need until time for the champagne while hanging stockings for Santa."

1 quart fresh, select oysters	Worcestershire sauce
2 quarts milk	Tabasco sauce
1 pint light cream	Salt
Onion juice	Pepper

"Bring oysters to a boil in their own liquor for two to three minutes. Add milk and cream; bring to boiling point, but do not boil. Season to taste with onion juice, Worcestershire sauce, a couple drops of Tabasco sauce, salt, and pepper. Serve with split common crackers, buttered and browned under a broiler.

"After the oyster stew, we always have a salad of Boston lettuce, avocado, grapefruit, and pomegranate seeds, with a light vinegar and oil dressing."

James (Jamie) Wyeth

Artist

*B*orn into an artistic family (his grandfather was N.C. Wyeth; his father, Andrew), Jamie Wyeth began his art training at an early age. Consequently, he had paintings hanging in permanent collections by the time he was 18, his first one-man show in New York City by age 20, and a retrospective before he was 30. In addition to an apartment in Manhattan and a farm in Chadds Ford, Pennsylvania, Jamie also owns a cottage on an island off the coast of Maine. "I spend half the year on Monhegan Island — a large part of that time is spent painting and eating periwinkles."

MONHEGAN ESCARGOT

"At dead low tide, gather half saucepan full of periwinkles and/or whelks — fill saucepan with sea water — chop and mix 2 cloves garlic with ¼ pound melted butter — boil snails ½ hour. To serve: provide diners with gold hatpin to remove snail from shell — discard black "door" of snail and dip in garlic butter!!!"

Index to People

Index to Recipes